STOKE MANDEVILLE
Where There's More Crows Than Folk

STOKE MANDEVILLE,

BUCKS,

A quarter of a mile from the Station, on the Metropolitan and Great Central Railways, whence Baker Street and Marylebone are reached in a few minutes over the hour; Two and a half miles from Aylesbury, the County Town of Bucks, with the Stations on the Metropolitan, Great Central, Great Western, and the London and North-Western Railways, the Great Central Expresses reaching London under the hour. London is 36 miles distant.

Particulars, Plan, and Conditions of Sale

OF

TWO FREEHOLD FARMS,

KNOWN RESPECTIVELY AS

STOKE HOUSE FARM,

WHICH COMPRISES

An Old-fashioned and very roomy House,

Excellent Range of Farm Buildings,

2 good Cottages,

Water Mill & Wheel, for driving Farm Machinery,

AND

180a. 2r. 20p. of exceptionally good Pasture

AND A

Small Portion of Arable Land,

ALSO

MALT HOUSE FARM,

COMPRISING A

Nice Old-fashioned Farm House & Buildings,

ALSO

38a. 0r. 5p. of excellent Pasture Land.

THE ABOVE PROPERTIES will be OFFERED BY AUCTION, by direction of the Trustees of the late Mrs. MARY BENNETT, by

---

Messrs. W. BROWN & CO.

At the "GEORGE" HOTEL, AYLESBURY,

On WEDNESDAY, JUNE 17, 1908,

At 3.30 for 4 precisely.

Particulars may be obtained of Messrs. J. & T. PARROTT, Solicitors, Aylesbury; and of the Auctioneers, Messrs. W. BROWN & CO., Tring (Tel. 11) and Aylesbury (Tel. 36); who will also give orders to view the Properties.

PRINTED BY O. T. DE FRAINE & CO., TRING AND AYLESBURY.

Auction details of Stoke House and Malt House Farms, 1908.

STOKE MANDEVILLE

Where There's More Crows Than Folk

Alan Dell &
Richard Pearce

Phillimore

1992

Published by
PHILLIMORE & CO. LTD.,
Shopwyke Hall, Chichester, Sussex

ISBN 0 85033 817 4

Printed and bound in Great Britain by
BIDDLES LTD.
Guildford, Surrey

Contents

List of Illustrations

Acknowledgements

Stuart Allen, 16, 17, 34; British Library Newspaper Library, 11; Bucks. County Museum, 38, 46, 47; Bucks. County Reference Library, 22-5; the *Bucks Herald*, 50, 55, 57; Bucks. Record Office, frontispiece (BRO. D/BML/19/18), 9 (BRO. DC2/37/2/11), 27 (BRO. DC2/37/2/11), 30 (BRO. DC2/37/2/11), 31 (BRO. DC2. 37/2/11), 32 (BRO. P/U A.27), 40 (BRO. DC2. 37/2/11), 48, 56 (BRO WIG/2/5/37); Mrs. S. Carter, 10, 18-21; Arthur Cutler, 13, 15, 41; Alan Dell, 39, 52; Mrs. M. Farnell, 3, 4, 6-8, 28, 29; John Jakobi, 49; The Rev. D. A. Johnson and Mrs. W. Chandler, 12, 36, 53; Midas Press, 45; Phillimore & Co. Ltd, 1; John Reed, 42, 43, 51; Royal Commission on Ancient Monuments, 5; The Misses Spencer, 58; Stoke Mandeville Parish Council, 26; Stoke Mandeville Women's Institute, 37; Mrs. N. Tapping, 2, 44; Tom Taylor, 35; Mrs. P. Vernon, 14, 54.

Foreword

The joint authors of this book felt that, with the formation of the Stoke Mandeville and Other Parishes Charity in 1986, which it is hoped will bring great benefits to Stoke Mandeville parish in future years, an up-to-date history of the parish should be compiled from 1797. Thanks to the sponsorship of the charity this has now been made possible.

Stoke Mandeville has never been part of a large landed estate nor has it had a wealthy lord of the manor. Accordingly, early history of the village is very sketchy and documentation sparse, and the only other written work on the parish was compiled by E. R. Matthaei in his *History of Stoke Mandeville* published in 1955. Much of this modest work consisted of verbatim extracts from Lipscombe's massive *History of the County of Buckinghamshire* (1837) and Sheehan's *History and Topography of the County of Buckinghamshire* (1871).

So why is 1797 a starting date? In that year Parliament passed the Stoke Mandeville Enclosure Act which came into force on 13 September 1798. At that time a detached part of the parish of some 130 acres was at Prestwood and nearly four acres of gravel-bearing land there was awarded to the Surveyors of the Highway of Stoke Mandeville for the upkeep of the parish roads. This land was never sold and, although there were several references to it in the minutes of the Stoke Mandeville Parish Council (formed in 1894), that body had completely forgotten about its existence until their attention was drawn to it by Richard Pearce of Moat Farm.

The story of how this re-discovery eventually led to the Charity Commissioners setting up the Stoke Mandeville and Other Parishes Charity, and of the subsequent windfall, is told in the ensuing pages, as are some of the stories of former times showing the villagers at work and at play. These have been compiled from many sources too numerous to list.

The joint authors hope that this book will be of interest not only to the present inhabitants of the parish and neighbourhood but for generations to come.

TERRA EPI LINCOLIENSIS. *In Elesberie HD*

ⓜ REMIGIVS eps Lincoliæ teñ STOCHES . ꝓ vĩii . hiđ
se defđ . Tra . ē . xxi . car . In dñio . iii . hidæ . 7 ibi funt
vi . car . Ibi . xx . uilli cũ . iiii . borđ hñt . xv . car . Ibi . iii .
ferui . 7 i . moliñ de . x . fol . Silua . xxx . porc . Ptũ . iii . car .
Hoc ⓜ jacet ad æcclam de Elesberie . Ibi . xviii . borđ
qui reddunt ꝓ annũ . xx . fol . In totis ualent ual . xx .
liɓ . Q̃do recep . xii . liɓ . T.R.E. xviii . liɓ . Hoc ⓜ cũ
æccla tenuit Wluui eps T.R.E. De . viii . hund ꝗ jaceɴ
in circuitu Elefberie . unufꝗ́fꝗ fochs qui hĩ . i . hidã
aut plus . redđ unã fumã annonæ huic æcclæ . Adhuc
etiã de unoꝗꝗ focho . i . aĉ annonæ aut . iiii . denarij
foluebant huic æcclæ T.R.E. fed poft aduentũ regis . W.
redditũ non fuit.

1. Stoke Mandeville's entry in Domesday Book, 1086.

[3a]   **LAND OF THE BISHOP OF LINCOLN**

In AYLESBURY Hundred

1   M. REMIGIUS Bishop of Lincoln holds STOKE (Mandeville).
It answers for 8 hides. Land for 21 ploughs; in lordship 3
hides; 6 ploughs there.
     20 villagers with 4 smallholders have 15 ploughs.
     3 slaves; 1 mill at 10s; woodland, 30 pigs; meadow for 3 ploughs.
This manor lies with the (lands of) Aylesbury Church.
     18 smallholders who pay 20s a year.
Total value £20; when acquired £12; before 1066 £18.
     Bishop Wulfwy held this manor with the church before 1066.
From the eight hundreds which lie in the circuit of Aylesbury, each
Freeman who has 1 hide or more pays one load of corn to this
church. Furthermore from each Freeman 1 acre of corn or 4d was
paid over to this church before 1066, but after the coming of King
William it was not paid.

X

Setting the Record Straight

As so little documented history of Stoke Mandeville survives from before the late 18th century, some unsubstantiated stories have appeared in print from time to time. This book provides the opportunity to try to set the record straight.

An example of inaccuracy even appears in the *Victoria County History of Buckinghamshire* where the date of the new church is given as 1886 instead of 1866 – a pure misprint. But since then nearly every reference made to St Mary's has compounded the error. These have ranged from the celebrated Professor Pevsner in the *Buildings of England* series to the recent museum report on the Stoke ruins.

Another oft-repeated myth is that the Brudenell children, Mary, Thomas and Dorothy, whose respective deaths are recorded on the family monument, were killed by Cromwellian soldiers. The date on the memorial has been estimated by experts in that field as about 1584, 15 years before Cromwell's birth, so whatever 'mortal blades' cut down the children, this could not have been the work of his soldiers and is more likely to have been an illness which decimated the family. (The sculptor is thought to have created a similar monument of this date in Ellesborough church.)

Lipscombe in his work on Buckinghamshire states of the old church that 'the original tower and north aisle were demolished by violence'. This has led others to write that the church tower was destroyed by Cromwell's soldiers during the Civil War. It is known that Aylesbury was garrisoned by his troops during this conflict and there is reason to believe that some were billeted in Stoke Mandeville, but the church tower would have been a splendid look-out position for the soldiers over the flat countryside of the Vale and its demolition for any reason is entirely undocumented. It would have been quite illogical in the circumstances, particularly as the war was going the Parliamentarians' way.

Another piece of pure mythology concerns the piece of land for which John Hampden was summoned for non-payment of 20s. Ship Money. Arthur Mee's *Buckinghamshire* identifies this as Moat Farm in Marsh Lane, Stoke Mandeville (once owned by Richard Pearce, the co-author of this record). Quite where this information came from is not known but, of course, once in print the story sticks and is repeated even though the name of Moat Farm has only recently been given to the property. In former times it was called Lower, or Brook Close Farm. Parts of it are the oldest building in the village. If a Moat Farm was involved in this particular story, it is more likely to have been the one at Prestwood, about a mile and a half from the family home at Great Hampden. Others suggest that it was a wood on which the tax was levied.

So the moral is that, wherever possible, the original sources of information and reference should be looked at.

Some Important Dates in Stoke Mandeville's History

1045-65	The Manor of Stoke in the hands of Bishop Wulfwy of Dorchester.
1066	William the Conqueror passes close to Stoke with his retinue, which included Geoffroi de Mandeville, on his way to receive the submission of the Saxon leaders of Berkhamsted Castle. Another 200 years are to pass before the name Mandeville is associated with Stoke.
1086	Stoke (Stoches) mentioned in Domesday Book. Total value £20, when acquired £12; before 1066, £18. 1254 Geoffrey de Mandeville holds the whole of Stoke.
1294	A chaplain appointed for Stoke by the Bishop of Lincoln.
1409	Henry Brudenell of Aynho possessed of the Manor of Oldbury in Stoke.
1601	Francis Brudenell possessed of the Manor of Newbury in Stoke.
1635	John Hampden, the Patriot, refuses to pay 20s. Ship Money on his property in Stoke Mandeville parish.
1639	Edmund Brudenell sells the Manors of Oldbury and Newbury.
1645	Parliamentary soldiers billeted in the village; 'A heavy burden on the countryside'.
1726	Jackson's Charity established.
1733	Ligo's Charity established.
1790	Charles Lucas becomes lord of the manor.
1798	Parish enclosed by Act of Parliament.
1815	Methodist chapel founded.
1827	Repairs made to St Mary's church.
1858	Stoke Mandeville is detached from Bierton parish and the first vicar is appointed.
1866	The new church of St Mary's is consecrated.
1868	Methodist chapel rebuilt.
1884	The detached portion of the parish at Prestwood transferred out of Stoke.
1892	Metropolitan Railway comes to Stoke.
1894	Stoke Mandeville Parish Council established.
1895	The Board School opens.
1903	Mains water laid to the village.
1908	John Henry Tapping becomes lord of the manor.
1934	Stoke streets lit by electricity.
1950	Mains drainage comes to the village.
1958	The new Methodist church opens.
1978	Stoke Mandeville Village Community Centre opens.
1986	Stoke Mandeville and Other Parishes Charity established.

Chapter One

The Prestwood
Its lands, owners and the formation of the charity

Prestwood, in Stoke Mandeville, belonged to the Hampden family as far back as the 13th century and it was later to become famous, by tradition, as the piece of land on which John Hampden refused to pay ship money of 20s. in 1635.

Like his father, who was said to have been the wealthiest commoner in the land, owning property in three counties, and his grandfather, John Hampden was a member of Parliament. He was first elected for the Cornish seat of Grampound in 1621 during the reign of King James, although he was without west country connections. Subsequently he put up for Wendover and later Buckingham, and he was imprisoned, more than once, for refusing to pay taxes levied by the king without the authority of Parliament.

Approximately ten years later the king repeated his tax raising exercise. This time he levied ship money which, as a special one-off tax, he considered could be dealt with under the Royal prerogative. This ancient tax had, by tradition, been imposed upon coastal towns and counties in times of danger for the protection of such places by the Navy, but never before had it been extended inland. Hampden's refusal to pay was treated as a test case, but when the Court of Exchequer found by a majority against him, the country at large thought otherwise.

It has proved impossible to identify the precise piece of land on which the charge remained unpaid. Both he and thirty or so other parishioners at Great Kimble where he owned more land declined to pay, although he paid up for Great Hampden without apparent protest. In the indictment records, however, John Hampden appears as 'of Stoke Mandeville' and Prestwood was, at that time, within the parish close to the family home at Great Hampden. When the final writ for non-payment was made in October 1636, the Stoke Mandeville land seems to have been chosen almost by chance.

Six years later, in 1642, King Charles failed in his attempt to arrest six of the Parliamentary leaders, one of whom was Hampden, and this caused the King to quit the capital and set up his standard at Oxford.

The following year, during a minor skirmish with the Royalist army just outside the village of Chalgrove near Thame in Oxfordshire, Hampden was fatally wounded in the shoulder, dying six days later. The wound was attended to by a Mr. Delafield, surgeon to the Thame garrison, who later came to live in Aylesbury.

The cause of death of 'the Patriot', as Hampden's followers dubbed him, has often been disputed for, in another version of the incident, a pistol which was one of a pair given to him by his son-in-law, Sir Robert Pye, was said to have burst as Hampden discharged it. Such was the interest in the manner of his death, that 185 years later an effort was made to clear up the mystery once and for all by exhuming the body. With the agreement of Hampden's descendant the Earl of Buckingham, George Lord Nugent, one of the two members of Parliament for Aylesbury with a party of grave-diggers and onlookers acting as helpers, undertook this gruesome task on 21 July 1828 and a very full account of the proceedings was taken at the time.

To begin with there had never been a Hampden ancestral vault in the Great Hampden church and all the family burials had taken place in the chancel. Several leaden coffins were examined and one was selected, but the corroded name plate crumbled as soon as it was touched. Nevertheless it was decided to open it as that of Hampden. No firm decision could be reached as to whether there had been a gun shot wound in the shoulder but upon further examination the right hand was found to have been amputated, the bones of the severed hand resting in a separate cloth. Thus it was concluded by the onlookers that the story of the exploding pistol was a valid one and that Hampden had not been wounded by a Royalist soldier.

Although a full account of the exhumation was reported in the paper at the time, when Lord Nugent came to publish his *Life of Hampden*, all these details were suppressed as it was subsequently asserted that the body in question was not that of Hampden but of a female, and the bones mistaken for those of an amputated hand were in fact those of a infant, 'the lady having died durante partu', in childbirth.

In 1863 a memorial was erected near Honor End Farm by Judge Erle on which appears this inscription:

FOR THESE LANDS IN STOKE MANDEVILLE
JOHN HAMPDEN
WAS ASSESSED TWENTY SHILLINGS
SHIP MONEY LEVIED BY COMMAND OF THE KING
WITHOUT AUTHORITY OF LAW
THE 4TH AUGUST 1635. BY RESISTING THIS CLAIM OF THE KING
IN LEGAL STRIFE
HE UPHELD THE RIGHT OF THE PEOPLE
UNDER THE LAW
AND BECAME ENTITLED TO GRATEFUL REMEMBERANCE HIS WORK ON
EARTH ENDED AFTER THE CONFLICT IN CHALGROVE FIELD
THE 24TH JUNE 1643
AND HE RESTS IN GREAT HAMPDEN CHURCH.

As has been mentioned, the site of the piece of land for which the ship money was not paid is now disputed and the position of the memorial is said to have been chosen because of its close proximity to Hampden House. The story of the unpaid ship money does not, however, end there for another, less well-known landowner, who can positively be identified within Stoke Mandeville, also defaulted.

Alexander Jennings, who was in possession of the Manors of Burleys and Stonors and assessed for £25 17s. 9d., refused to pay and this brought him into conflict with the authorities. The Privy Council messenger detained Jennings for 19 weeks at Oatlands, one of the King's palaces near Weybridge in Surrey, and then conducted him to the Fleet Prison until he produced a certificate of payment for Stoke Mandeville.

After 12 weeks in the Fleet, Jennings petitioned for release so that he could attend to his affairs and especially 'remove himself from the contagion in the city'. The messenger complained 'Jennings runs every week to the carriers and receives letters from the country. If there is no stricter warrant for restraining him, he will never pay his Majesty nor the writer'. The Star Chamber wrote to the Warden of the Fleet Prison in May 1638 instructing him to detain Jennings until further notice, 'as he has used scandalous speeches in derogation of his Majesty's Government'.

The other inhabitants of Stoke Mandeville saw fit to pay their dues although undoubtedly not without complaint. Headed by Mr. Edmund Brudenell, at £2 2s. 6d., 12 landowners paid a total of just in excess of £11. Why Jennings's sum was so much higher is not clear unless it was because of his position as lord of the manors; nor is it clear whether another petition in 1639 was successful, for after this his name drops out of the State Papers. Often only half the story is revealed in the records. Jennings died in 1645 but was not buried in the parish.

Before 1849, because 'The Prest Wood' was a full six miles from St Mary's at Stoke Mandeville, it was more practical and convenient for the handful of folk who lived in the detached part of the parish to be ministered to by the clergy in adjacent parishes. Thus, particularly in Great Hampden, there is a sprinkling of entries in the registers for Stoke folk. Baptisms were performed and recorded with remarks such as '... in regard of ye farre journey to their owne parish Church' or 'upon leave because of ye farr distance fro' their church'.

The new parish of Prestwood was created in April 1852 by Order in Council out of parts of the ecclesiastical parishes of Hughenden, Great Missenden and Stoke Mandeville. Its church of Holy Trinity was consecrated in 1849. Thirty-six years later, in March 1885, the detached portion belonging to Stoke Mandeville which consisted of land totalling 175 acres including Kiln Common, cottages in Honor End Lane, Bottom Farm and Honor End Farm, was attached for civil purposes to Great and Little Hampden parishes.

Secondary roads, as distinct from those which were controlled and managed by the various turnpike trusts and on which a toll was levied for traffic other than pedestrians, were the responsibility of each parish. At every Quarter Sessions, a part of the proceedings was given over to highway matters and the magistrates maintained general supervision.

They appointed Surveyors of the Highway for each parish and then it was up to the individual parish to look after matters to the best of their ability. But, of course, in the days before Mr. McAdam had appeared on the scene, gravel was needed – hence the provision in every enclosure act for a gravel pit. Thus the Surveyors of the Highway for Stoke Mandeville parish were allotted a gravel outcrop to help with the upkeep of the parish roads, which were over 28 acres in area. Unemployed men in the parish were sent to dig gravel there and were paid a pittance for their trouble. They were expected to dig a yard of gravel for a day's pay. This was in the days before unemployment pay had ever been heard of.

A glance at the Surveyors of the Highway account book shows that, as far as actual work on the roads was concerned, it had been agreed in the early part of the last century that the men were to work at Prestwood 'from 9 o'clock till half past 2 o'clock' whilst the men at Stoke 'from half past six till 5'. This five-hour difference in the working day is explained by the two and a half hours walking each way through the lanes to and from work. In 1835 yearly disbursements came to £19 4s. 2d. and the daily rate varied from 8d. to 10d. per man.

When the rural district councils took over the upkeep of parish roads, and later, in the first decade of this century 'dole money' started to be paid, interest in gravel digging waned and for more than 60 years the existence of the pit was forgotten. In January 1906 the parish council considered Mr. Lazenby-Liberty's request to purchase land at Prestwood. It seems there were others in the bidding and the council, realising the land's potential for building purposes, were of the opinion that it should not be sold unless its special value as such was reflected in the price. After some haggling, negotiations seem to have been terminated as the sale did not proceed.

In 1908 Great and Little Hampden Parish Council asked whether the council would be willing to let out the remaining Prestwood land for allotments. In its reply the council were of the opinion that the value of the land would be depreciated by its being broken up. At this point all mention of the land drops out of the minute books but from other sources it is clear that in about 1921 it was let out to the Great Missenden Parish Council for allotment purposes at £4 per annum. This rent was paid to Stoke Mandeville Parish Council for 65 years without anyone really being aware of what the sum, later increased to £100 per annum, represented.

Thanks to the assiduous research of Councillor Richard Pearce, the ownership of the same land was re-established, the Charity Commissioners being satisfied that it belonged to the parish of Stoke Mandeville. The Stoke Mandeville and Other Parishes Charity was constituted on 11 November 1986 and it was duly confirmed that the land in question was the sole property of the charity.

The rest is well known. Part of the land was sold for building purposes and the proceeds invested, Stoke Mandeville getting, via the trustees, ten-elevenths of the investment income with Great Hampden and Great Missenden sharing the remaining eleventh. It is hoped that the income arising from the investments will bring great benefits to the inhabitants of the parish in future years.

Chapter Two

The Parish Council and School Land

The first meeting of the Stoke Mandeville Parish Council was held in the National Schoolroom near the vicarage on Tuesday 4 December 1894 at 6.30 p.m. It had been called, after due notice, under the parish councillor's Election Order 1894 and a circular letter of instructions had been received from the Local Government Board via the parish overseers.

This order was part of the reform of local government which had been undertaken in the last three decades of the century. School Boards had been set up in 1870 followed by the Public Health Act five years later, which had created urban and rural district sanitary districts.

In 1888 the authority of the Justices of the Peace over administration ceased and the government of the counties, apart from the police, was put in the hands of the county councils, and the new urban and district councils were given certain powers in their own right. The latter act converted the sanitary districts into districts *per se*. Each rural parish of over 300 souls was required to elect a council and those of less than that number were to hold a parish meeting, the former consisting of elected members and the latter of ratepayers. Stoke Mandeville was in the first category and, when the nomination papers were handed in, there were 10 proposals for the five seats. One candidate received only one vote, and he demanded and got a poll. The clerk's salary was agreed at £2 10s. per annum.

In 1896 moves were afoot to move the parish out of the High Wycombe union into that of Aylesbury and a special meeting was called on 1 May to discuss the matter. It was a logical suggestion, for Aylesbury was but a short drive for councillors and other parish officials, whereas the journey to Saunderton, where the meetings took place, was extremely difficult by road in the winter and the train had to be taken at Aylesbury or Kimble.

The request was turned down by the Wycombe Board of Guardians but by such a small majority (15 to 14) that the parish decided to pursue the matter and seek the support of the county council. In the meantime the Stoke representative on the Wycombe rural district council, who was also the local vicar, was less than helpful to the cause when he implied that the parish had changed its mind now that a station was being built nearer the Saunderton Union house. This was only another chapter in the long running battle of wills between this gentleman and parishioners. The county, however, was on the side of the parish and made the necessary order for the transfer in May 1897. Although the Wycombe rural district council petitioned against it, a local enquiry later in the year confirmed the order.

In the early days when the councillors were keen to exercise their newly won authority, meetings were held every month and well attended, although in 1897 the rule concerning non attendance for six months was exercised and the man concerned was declared to have vacated his seat (The Local Government Act 1894 Section 46 Paras. 6 & 7).

By 1921 meetings were only being held two or three times a year and during the Second World War twice a year was the norm. As the war ended, however, the need for more frequent meetings became evident. Some councillors favoured once a month, whilst the chairman proposed every six weeks. The clerk said he could not possibly attend more than quarterly and unless the council agreed to this, he would be forced to tender his resignation after 30 years in the job. The vacant post was duly advertised.

A proposal in the early 1930s to transfer the parish into the borough of Aylesbury was opposed by residents. The Local Government Act of 1929 had recommended an adjustment of boundaries where this would improve village facilities and the county proposed extending the borough to include the villages of Stoke Mandeville, Weston Turville, Aston Clinton and Bierton.

The resolution from a meeting of the villagers in January 1931 made it clear that they were opposed to the plan in that 'the present growth of the borough does not warrant it taking in the rural parish of Stoke Mandeville and that the rural district council can provide all the services necessary or required more economically than the borough'. They were also unhappy at what they saw as wasteful projects being undertaken by the borough including the new Vale Recreation Ground to which they would have to contribute through the rates without any benefit to the village. The desirability of maintaining the parish's separate indentity from its ever expanding neighbour has lasted to the present day. Mr. John Henry Tapping held the position of chairman of the council from its inception until 1910 when, upon his proposition, the vicar, Frederick Winterton, was appointed to succeed him. A full list of those who have served the community as chairmen and clerks to the Stoke Mandeville Parish Council appears at the end of this chapter.

It is interesting to note how some of the parish officers established under earlier legislation remained in place, at least in name, until comparatively recently. It seemed that the parish clerk's job always carried with it that of assistant overseer of the poor whilst the annual appointment of the two parish constables lasted up to 1947 when it was dropped 'as redundant'. The latter position was finally abolished by the Police Act 1964.

The historic post of parish constable lost most of its authority when the police force was formed in the last century. Even then it appears to have carried with it a certain kudos for there were quite a few vying for the job in the early days of the council. The holder of the office was able, at his discretion, to detain a parishioner for any wrong doing, a forerunner, perhaps of the present day 'citizen's arrest'. This was a complete turnabout from the days when the office of constable carried with it a heavy workload of usually unpopular duties for then, when the turn came to serve, the job was not welcomed and the practice of paying someone else to do it was widespread. One of the statutory functions of the parish council has been to administer the parish allotments. It will be seen in another chapter that allotments were allocated to labourers in an effort to alleviate hardship brought about by parish enclosures, and a 40-acre field in Marsh Lane, known as Bradleys and just outside the parish boundary, was set aside and divided into acre plots. There was no water on this site so it had to be carried from the brook in Marsh Lane.

At the turn of the century it was more convenient to have these plots nearer the village, and the owner of the land, Lord Rothschild, at the same time, transferred them to another field of his behind the school. They were also, at the same time, much reduced in size.

Directly after the First World War, when the demand for plots was probably at its height, Lord Rothschild's agent was instructed to offer for sale for £400 seven acres of the allotments to the parish council. A loan was agreed and the price was adjusted to £350. Rents were costed at 9d. per pole and the clerk was paid £2 per annum for their collection, although another five years went by before the purchase was completed. In 1928 the owner of the adjoining Manor Cottage asked if he could have a half-acre portion of the land to extend his garden, and after a delay of four years this was agreed at a figure of £125.

In 1954 the council was asked to sell just under an acre of the allotments to extend the school field and, as plots were vacant, the councillors voiced no opposition. The district valuer was asked to work out a price and £1,200 was agreed. Fifteen years later another one and a half acres was required for further expansion of the school and the district valuer was again asked to act for the parish council. This time some building was to take place on the site and councillors were of the opinion that, whilst the plot in 1954 was sold as agricultural land, there was a case to be made this time for the valuation to reflect the changed circumstances.

There then ensued five years of protracted negotiations over the value of the land culminating in an appeal to the Department of the Environment by the parish council over the amount of compensation due. Permission to build six houses on the site had been granted in an effort to establish the true value of the land. This bore fruit when a figure of nearly £100,000, including interest, was awarded. The bulk of this sum was used to build the present Community Centre.

Chapter Three

The Old Church

The original Norman parish church of St Mary's stood about a thousand yards to the south-east of the present church, towards Terrick not far from Stoke House. Its site, a ruin of overgrown rubble, can still be visited by the inquisitive but this is hardly worth the effort other than as a curiosity, although there are plans to make the place more accessible. The old church was abandoned as a place of worship after the move to the new site. It has been described as containing a small Norman nave and chancel, the latter being lengthened in the 13th century. The south aisle was added in the next century whilst another century was to pass before the nave walls were raised and the low-pitched roof put on. The brick tower on the western end was a later addition. Extensive repairs were required in 1827 after a spate of lead stripping from the roof. Two years earlier a charge had been brought against three men for such an offence but they were discharged for lack of evidence. Apparently stripping off lead from church roofs is not only a 20th-century phenomenon.

Lipscombe in his work on Buckinghamshire describes the church as 'standing in a watery meadow south of the village' and when Robert Gibbs wrote of the place in his *History of Aylesbury*, he said it was 'in a damp, inconvenient and secluded spot, no longer used for regular worship'. Interestingly his own remains lie in the selfsame secluded spot. His wife, Mary (1826-75), who was the daughter of Thomas Gurney of Whitethorn House, is in the same grave although Robert Gibbs outlived her by nearly 20 years. As late as 1908, 42 years after it ceased to be a place of worship, burials were still taking place in family graves in the old churchyard and some dozen or so tombstones can still be viewed by the inquisitive and active visitor.

Why was it found necessary to build a new church? The drift of the village northwards from the marshy site which had served the population for eight centuries seems to have been the final arbitrator and when the Risborough Road, which formerly ran close to the church and Stoke House, was realigned to the west, a more convenient spot nearer Aylesbury was chosen for the new building.

It was not long before a slow deterioration of the old church set in and the decaying site soon became a playground for the mischievous. There is an interesting account in a local paper of 1867, shortly after the church was abandoned, of 'A Christmas Frolic in the Church' which led to an unfortunate prosecution

2. Old St Mary's church from a painting owned by Mrs. N. Tapping.

3. Old St Mary's church, south view.

by the authorities. Before the court were seven young people charged with maliciously damaging a window in the church, the estimated repair being put at 15s. One of the youngsters had been persuaded to give evidence against his companions and stated that he had been with them in the old church between midnight and one o'clock on the morning of Christmas Day (1866). They had had some beer to drink and some 'hot-potch'. One of the lads broke a window and climbed through, unfastening the door to let in the rest. Then they started to ring the bells and continued to do so until three in the morning when they went home.

A churchwarden, Mr. Bennett of Stoke House, stated that his attention was called to the state of the window on Christmas morning. Soon after midnight on Christmas Eve he heard the parties going past his house and soon afterwards heard the bells ringing and this continued until four in the morning.

The bench asked whether it was not the custom to ring the bells on such occasions, to which the churchwarden replied that they had not been rung for a long time. The church was closed to the public and there was no necessity to open it unless the clergyman had to perform any services there. There was only one bell in the new church but there had never before been any depredation to the building. The church was complete except the flooring and a few pews with fittings left there so that services could be conducted if the parishioners preferred it to the new church.

The defending solicitor suggested that the only object of the defendants was to have a little Christmas frolic and they did not intend to commit any damage. Ringing bells was customary at that festive season and as there were no bells in the new church, they proceeded to the old one and had the fun of a peal or two. It would have been more seemly if the vicar, Mr. Partington, had sent for them and remonstrated with them for their conduct. The voluntary repair of the window would have met the justice of the case rather than seeking to fine or imprison them for what was really only a seasonal prank.

A fine of 12s. was imposed on each of the five boys and they were ordered to pay the amount of the damage between them, in default of 14 days' imprisonment. This seemingly harsh fine did little to enhance the vicar's reputation in the village, and was the forerunner of more unpleasant incidents within the next few years involving at least one of these boys.

Some years later a vivid description of the ruinous building was given in a letter to both of the local papers by Mr. Charles Strachey of Terrick House, in an effort to bring to the notice of the public the sad state of affairs at that time including the possible destruction, through neglect, of the ancient Brudenell monument.

Dated 12 August 1898, Mr. Strachey wrote :

The outer fabric of the church appears – to one without any special knowledge – to be, as yet, fairly sound and the churchyard seems to be kept in good order. But the windows are broken, ivy has crept INSIDE the building, and it is pretty to see the swallows darting up and down the arches of the nave. Ceilings and woodwork are, of course, crumbling and collapsing; bits of old pews and worm eaten doors and shutters lie tumbled about with other ecclesiastical wreckage in various stages of decay: here a rickety wooden pulpit on its side; there a broken desk or book rest to which scraps of red cloth still adhere.

The floor is strewn with plaster, broken glass and loose rubble of all kinds, and the columns and arches are scrawled over with names and dates, from which it may be gathered that the place is a common resort, especially at Bank Holiday time, of persons whose motives for visiting it are neither religious, archaeological, nor artistic. Access is easy at present. The chancel door stands open but it should be locked. A ready means of entry is provided by a broken window, the ledge of which is very conveniently near the ground.

4.   Interior of old St Mary's church, looking east.

The vicar of the parish, which is a very poor one, informs me that he has repeatedly, and at his own expense, attempted to protect the building from damage from man and by the weather, but that he finds it impossible to do so. He also tells me that sacrilegious invaders have actually tried to disturb the tombs, of which the heraldic slabs are still decipherable among the dust and dilapidation of the floor.

The letter had the required effect insofar as the monument was concerned, for it was removed to the new church the following year by the fifth Marquess of Ailesbury, the then head of the Brudenell family.

Mr. Strachey's letter was received with concern by local antiquarians, and certainly when 'An Old Boy' joined the correspondence 10 days later he was of the opinion that it was incredible that so deplorable a state of affairs should exist in 'this enlightened age'. As events had proved, he said, the erection of the new church had been a great mistake and if the money and labour spent on the new church had been devoted to repairing the old one and a good path across the fields, it would still be a thing of beauty and a joy for ever. He appealed for funds to rectify the position adding that 'the price of a racehorse would save the church from destruction'.

Mr. John Parker, secretary of the Buckinghamshire Archaeological Society, was asked by the Society of Antiquaries to make a report and his recommendations were radical:

A strong effort should be made (after the renovation of the old church and construction of a good dry gravel path across the fields) to induce parishioners to go back to their old parish church so full of memories of the past and convert the present church, which is evidently not a costly construction, into a building for the intellectual advantage and social happiness of the community.

An attempt was also made to clear the interior and to bring about 'some appearance of order' but nothing more positive was attempted.

In 1908, however, the Archdeacon of Buckingham urged that something should be done to save the chancel arch, and the same year the Vestry decided that, to combat the thefts of lead from the roof, the rest of it should be removed and sold. This action, which on the face of it contradicted the earlier suggestion, was said to have been made with the cordial approval of the bishop but merely hastened rapid deterioration. When, three years later, the ruined building was the subject of a report to the Committee of the Society for the Preservation of Ancient Buildings, it was stated that the nave 'was open to the weather' and that it should be covered with corrugated galvanized iron.

This suggestion evoked a storm of protest from the Committee and certainly photographs taken in the 1930s show that this was not carried out, although some of the graves were still tended. The then owner of Stoke House,

5. Old St Mary's church, 'open unto the sky'.

Mr. R. S. King-Farlow, is said to have instructed his farm bailiff, Charlie Collins, to mow the grass and keep the churchyard tidy as and when he could during working hours. Someone still cared.

Nevertheless as a playground for mischievous, or some would say adventurous, youth it continued to be a worry to the authorities and this was compounded in 1937 when a 14-year-old lad, William Stainton, was killed by a fall of masonry. It seems from the report of the inquest that he and his two companions had been playing in the ruins when the accident occurred.

Considerable criticism was levelled at the church authorities for leaving a building in such a dangerous condition and open to all. As a result further efforts were made to secure the building from intruders but none was very successful. Shortly after this Stoke House was sold and there was no one left to keep the paths tidy, and nettles and weeds took over.

In 1964 the parish council drew the Church authorities' attention to the ruinous and dangerous condition of the church and suggested that demolition was the only answer. The parochial church council agreed and on 21 January 1966 this short report appeared in the *Bucks Herald*:

> The remains of the church of St Mary the Virgin, which have stood in the grounds of Stoke House, Stoke Mandeville for more than 50 years, were finally demolished on Sunday by a troop of the Royal Engineers of the Territorial Army. The remains of the church were winched down at the request of the parochial church council.

So ended 800 years of history.

Chapter Four

The New Church

The present church of St Mary the Virgin was built in 1865-6. The foundation stone was laid by the bishop of Oxford, Samuel Wilberforce, the son of the anti-slavery campaigner, William Wilberforce, on 25 April 1865 and the completed building was consecrated by Bishop Wilberforce on 9 July the following year.

The need for a radical look at the parish was evident 20 years earlier as the Letter Books of the same bishop make clear. Writing in 1847 to the Dean and Chapter of Lincoln when Stoke Mandeville was still under the auspices of the vicar of Bierton, Bishop Samuel said:

> In Stoke Mandeville the Chapter possess about 150 acres of good land worth £250 per annum. The Vicarial Tythes are £70. If the Chapter will assist this income there is a strong desire in the parish to obtain a resident clergyman and much help would be rendered towards building a glebe house. The present spiritual condition of the parish is very bad.

A farm building, later known as Stoke Farm, was erected shortly afterwards on this land and was sold by the Church authorities in 1880 to Geoffrey Gadsden of Weston Turville.

It was another 11 years before the first vicar was appointed and another five before the vicarage was ready, but it is clear that Charles Partington was a man of some energy. The access to the old church had become so difficult, especially for the old and infirm, that something had to be done, and quickly. In 1851 they had tried holding a service in the schoolroom but this had been a near disaster when the whole village tried to pack into such a small room: '... the heat and atmosphere of the place was injurious to the health of both preachers and hearers'.

The architect of the new church was James Redland Taylor, and the builder, T. Fitkin of Weston Turville. The cost of the whole project, including the land which was part of a close called the Green or Malthouse Green, owned by William Nansom Lettsom of Paddington, was £1,300. (He also owned the nearby Malthouse Farm and his grandfather was Dr. Lettsom, an eminent physician and co-helper with William Neild, the prison reformer.)

Nearly half the cost had been raised by the villagers themselves, and this in itself was quite remarkable as Stoke was a poor place. On the day of the consecration only £90 remained to be raised. The vicar and his young wife had been instrumental in raising £80 towards the building fund and, in particular, Mrs. Partington had organised 'a shilling for a church' scheme which involved public contributions of at least this sum from each person. Even the poorest villagers were keen to be involved so that they might be said to 'possess a brick' in the new church. Donations were also made by the Incorporated Church and Diocesan Church Building Societies.

Even for those days £1,300 was very little to pay for such a building and, as it turned out, corners had been cut during construction. It had been built with a

6. St Mary's church, c.1865.

7. The 15th-century font at St Mary's.

quadrilateral tiled roof which made the transfer of the five bells from the old church tower most difficult, and two of the bells had to be hung above a lower row of three. When another bell was added in 1910, the result was catastrophic for the four-sided roof began to sway every time the bells were rung and it even moved in high winds. Early in the 1920s it was dismantled and the tower reconstructed: later another two bells were added to bring the full complement to eight. Further trouble became apparent when the structure of the main fabric began to move. It was discovered that the church had been built without any real foundations and was slowly sinking. The remedial work necessary was carried out in the early 1930s entirely as a labour of love by a villager, Joseph Stilton, following his retirement from the railways at the age of 65. According to a glowing obituary notice in the *Bucks Herald*, written by the then vicar, singlehanded he underpinned the whole of the building with ferro-concrete, and the task took him three years.

Apart from the bells, what else found its way to the new church when the old one was abandoned? Most of the moveable fittings were taken across including the 15th-century font, a full description of which can be found in the *Victoria County History*: '... octagonal with square panels in the bowl ... the alternative panels contain a rose, a leaf pattern, a blank shield and what seems to be the representation of a shrine with a gabled top on which is a cresting of trefoil arches with a cross at either end'.

The ancient font cover was replaced within the last 20 years. The same work reports that 'a plated set of Communion vessels is in use. Other silver plate exists but cannot, it is alleged, be found and the registers are lost'. This particular point is discussed elsewhere in this book.

The pulpit was replaced and the ancient one found its way to Little Kimble church. Another item which did not reach the new church was the Illuminated Bell Board, the inscription on which read:

> He that turns a bell in this belforee
> Pays a groat to the Sexton, for that is his fee:
> and if you refuse your groat for to pay,
> The Churchwarden will your hat take away.

In 1942 the pulpit was again replaced – a gift from Miss Gosseling, a former resident of St Mary's Cottage. The same year the vicar's wife, Mrs. Winterton, donated an oak reading desk.

The Royal Coat of Arms painted on canvas and enclosed in a wooden frame stood over the chancel arch was also preserved in the new church. Until Victorian restoration most churches displayed such Arms; on plaster, carved in wood or painted on boards or canvas. It is currently being restored thanks to a grant from the Charity and when back in place will be one of only 60 or so still left in the county.

One prominent feature of the church is, of course, the Brudenell monument to which reference has already been made. The family were extensive land-owners in the area and possessed at least two Stoke manors from 1409 to 1639. Their monument, as has been seen, was rescued from the derelict church in 1899 by the Marquess of Ailesbury, the direct descendant of the earlier Brudenells, following concern in the local press on the danger of it being lost for ever.

Mr. Strachey's letter, quoted earlier in connection with the state of the old church, also described the condition of the monument in some detail:

In the scene of this desolation [the interior of the church] stands a monument ... the life-sized recumbent figure of a little girl, carved in white marble, in Eliza-bethan costume. The details of the dress, the lace ruff, the hair, etc. are treated with much delicacy: at the head of the figure are the effigies of two babies in swad-dling clothes; traces of colour are observable throughout. The rhymed inscription, unpolished in versification but touching in sentiment, tells us that this is the tomb of Mary, Thomas and 'Dorathy', children of Edmund Brudenell: Upon Good Fry-day at night my doll departed' and the like. If the Brudenell monument stood in a

8. The 16th-century Brudenell monument.

museum as an example of Elizabethan sculpture, it would receive ample attention. If it were in a village church in Normandy, it would be the pride of the place; tourists would visit it from the surrounding towns, and a café close by would drive a flourishing trade.

The sculptured figures have, of course, suffered from time to time from barbarism ... the fingers of the principal figure and the nose of one of the babies has lately been damaged and chipped; the fresh surface of the broken marble and the crumbled fragments lying there showed this without doubt. On the cheek of the little girl was a hard lump of red dust – some lighthearted vandal had thrown half a brick (there are plenty to hand) at her. Sooner or later – it is only a question of time – her head will be broken off and sold to some collector of curiosities in London. So will a fine example of the sculptor's art be lost for ever – sacrificed by indifference and cruel neglect.

Mr. Strachey's missive hit home and, with the agreement of the ecclesiastical authorities, the monument was established in the new church after 30 years of neglect. It was restored in 1985 in loving memory of William Eeley, churchwarden (1910-74). The full inscription on the Brudenell monument reads:

Cruell death by mortall blades
Hath slain foure of my tender babes
Whereof Mary Thomas and Dorathye
Within this place ther bodies lye
But God who never man deceaved
Hath ther soules to him receaved
This death to them is greatest gayne
Increasinge ther joy freeing them from payn
O Dorathye my blessed childe
Which lovingly lyved and dyed mylde
Thou wert my tenth even Gods own choys
In the excedingly I did rejoyse
Upon Good Fryday my doll depted
Adew my sweete and most true harted
My body with thyne I desyre should lye
When God hath appoynted me to dye
Hopeing thorough Christ he will provide
For my soule wthyne in haven to abyde
And I your father Edmunde Brudenell
Untill the resurrection wthe will dwell
And so adewe my sweete lambes three
Until in heaven I shall you see
Such is my hope of Richard my sonn
Whose body lyeth buryed in Kings Sutton

The church contains no other monuments. There is a grey stone tablet on the south wall near the door:

In Grateful memory of Frederick James Winterton
Vicar of this Parish 1908-51

His Care for his People was extended to Public Works
For Their Temporal Welfare as well as to the
Maintenance of this Church and Belfry

There is a small stained glass window in the lady chapel. On the south wall of the chancel there is a memorial window to Ernest Roger Matthaei (1884-1961) of Manor Cottage. A pencil drawing of the interior of the church in 1959 by J. Latimer stands on the window sill at the west end.

The baptistry was designed as a memorial to Robert Arthur Knight, church treasurer 1953-78, and on an adjacent window ledge stands a framed 'very old Chinese proverb':

> If there be righteousness in the heart,
> there will be beauty in the character.
> If there is beauty in the character,
> there will be harmony in the home.
> If there be harmony in the home,
> there will be order in the nation.
> When there is order in each nation,
> there will be peace in the world.

A village war memorial was first mooted in December 1919 after the signing of the peace terms earlier that year. A stone tablet was suggested as a suitable memorial and its position inside or outside the church became a matter of concern for Anglicans and Nonconformists alike. The former was decided upon and it was fixed to the north wall of the church.

1914-1918

Pte. C. KIDNEE	Pte. C. W. BUNCE
Gnr. W. E. EDWARDS	Pte. D. ROLFE
Pte. A. BUNCE	Pte. J. BRADLEY
Pte. A. J. PITCHER	Pte. J. SEAMONS
Gnr. E. BATEMAN	Gnr. A. SPITTLES

Names from the Second World War were added after that conflict and were also duplicated on another tablet within the Ex-Servicemen's Hall:

1939-1945

RONALD ALLEN	WILLIAM BATES
KENNETH HILL	RAYMOND MUNDAY
CHARLES PAYNE	HENRY THOMAS

> The Men were a wall unto us
> Both by Night and by Day.

The earliest registers have been lodged with the county archivist, whilst some of the later ones are still in the church.

The Vicars of St Mary the Virgin, Stoke Mandeville

The first vicar of the parish (1858-72) was Charles Edward PARTINGTON. Born in Manchester *c*.1826, he was the third son of James Edge Partington gent. and attended Manchester School. He entered Worcester College, Oxford in 1848. His curacies included Frodsham, Cheshire 1852-5 and Stand, Lancs. 1855-8. He married Miss Myfanwy Jane Kerr on 6 December 1859 at Twickenham parish church when she was eighteen.

Stoke Mandeville's new church was built during Mr. Partington's incumbency but his last days here were marred when, in 1871, he filed an unsuccessful petition for divorce against his wife on the grounds of adultery with a young man, Frederick James Townend. The village was badly split on the issue as two local young men, who were the chief witnesses, were subsequently convicted and jailed for perjury when the jury stopped the case. After this Mr. Partington left the parish and for 11 years went back to being a curate. He became Rector of Ambrose, Manchester in 1884 and died in 1897 at Rusholme near the same city.

The second vicar (1872-4) was Frederick Richard PENTREATH. Born in Cornwall *c*.1835, he was the eldest son of Richard Pentreath of Madron gent. He entered Exeter College, Oxford in 1853 and was Bible clerk at Worcester College 1854-6. Apart from his three years at Stoke, he held various school appointments between 1857-84 and for a year was Rector of Dodbrooke, Devon. He died at Bognor in 1894.

The third vicar (1874-9) was Edward Kingston HANSON. Born in Herefordshire in 1839, he was the second son of John Acton Hanson of Bunghill near Hereford. He entered Pembroke College, Oxford in 1858 and his curacies included Crewkerne 1863-5, Cromhall 1865-7, Stoke Orchard 1867-70, Alvington 1870-1 and, after leaving here, Nunton, Wiltshire 1880-3. He was vicar of Chepstow 1871-4 and of Maiden Bradley, Dorset 1883-96. He died in Dorset in 1906.

The fourth vicar (1879-1907) was Meyer MENSOR. Born *c*.1821 of Jewish parents, he attended the Royal Friedrich Wilhelm University and the Rabbinical College, Berlin (D.L. and D.Theo. in 1846) and for a time was Chief Rabbi in Chicago. He took up residence in Sheffield in January 1859, and, upon his conversion to Christianity, was baptised there in March 1861. His curacies included Pitmoor 1861-70, Jarrow 1870-2, Lynn Regis 1874-7, Norwich 1877-8 and Wenhaston, Suffolk 1878-9.

During his period at Stoke Mandeville, he was in constant dispute over the National School which, as sole manager, he failed to bring up to the standard required by government legislation due to lack of resources. He also appeared unable to retain the services of a schoolmaster for any length of time; again mostly because of the poor pay being offered.

He represented the parish on both the Wycombe and Aylesbury Rural District Councils and was the author of many theological tracts and papers.

9. The Rev. Frederick Winterton, *c.*1930, later to be called the 'Father of the Aylesbury Rural District Council'.

His wife, Annie, died on 8 May 1906 aged 89 and he remarried 10 weeks later after advertising for a housekeeper. A Church Commission of Enquiry investigated his neglect of duties including failure to take services, and he left the district just before the living was sequestrated in January 1907. He lived another seven years and died in poverty at the Hostel of God (now the Trinity Hospice) Clapham Common, London.

The fifth vicar (1908-51) was Frederick William WINTERTON. He attended Hatfield Hall, Durham, where he obtained his B.A. and between 1895-1902 was an assistant master at All Saints' School, Bloxham, during which time he was ordained. He was curate at St Mary's Bloxham, Banbury 1900-7.

Mr. Winterton represented the parish on the Aylesbury Rural District Council between 1908-51, serving as chairman 1929-32. As a result of his long tenure, he became known as the Father of the Council and only resigned due to ill health. He was also chairman of the parish council for 36 years.

In 1929 there was a vacancy on the county council following the elevation of Mr. A. Rose to the aldermanic bench and Mr. Winterton put himself forward to represent the joint villages of Bierton with Broughton, Weston Turville, Stone, Bishopstone, Hartwell, Hulcott and Stoke Mandeville. His opponents were Mr. Rupert East of Aylesbury and Mr. E. W. Clarke of Stone, a well-known member of the National Farmers' Union but Mr. Winterton topped the poll with 424 votes against Mr. Clarke's 334 and 136 for Mr. East. He became an alderman in 1934 and held the position for nearly two decades.

Mr. Winterton served the village through the changing years and is remembered with affection and respect. He died in 1953.

The sixth vicar (1952-62) was Hylton I'Brook SMITH. He attended Queen's College, Oxford and obtained his B.A. in 1920. He was curate of St Matthew's, Hammersmith 1923-4 and chaplain of St George's, Baghdad 1930-2. His incumbencies included Wyhen with Stoke Heath 1932-9, St Alban's, Stoke Heath 1939-40 and St John the Evangelist. Windermere 1940-52. After leaving Stoke Mandeville, he was vicar of Whaddon with Tottenhoe 1962-8, and he died in 1971.

The seventh vicar (1963-86) was Cyril John BURCH. He was at King's College, London in 1949 and his curacies included Milton Regis 1949-51, St Michael and All Angels, Croydon 1951-2, and was chaplain to various public schools before his move to Stoke Mandeville. He retired in 1986.

The eighth and present vicar (1989 to date), designated Rector of the joint benefices of Ellesborough, The Kimbles and Stoke Mandeville, is Samuel Frank Bruce HEYWOOD. After many years in the business world, he entered Oak Hill Theological College in 1979. He was curate at Chenies and Little Chalfont 1981-4, rector of Nash with Thornton, Beachampton and Thornborough, and rural dean of Buckingham in 1988 until his move to Stoke Mandeville.

Chapter Five

The National School

It was not until 1895, 25 years after the passing of the Act of Parliament which laid the foundations of state education in this country, that an effort was made to establish such a school in Stoke Mandeville. Until then education in the villages was mainly in the hands of the Church authorities and the records show that, certainly in Stoke Mandeville, perpetual underfunding prevented a coherent plan from being carried out.

The very earliest record of a school in the village was in 1819 when the vicar and curate of Bierton (until 1858 Stoke had no vicar of its own and was a chapelry of Bierton), together with six villagers, asked for it to be taken into the National Society, a London based organisation whose aims were '... the Promoting of Education of the Poor in the Principles of the Established Church'. This school's size and venue is unknown and 25 years were to pass before it was formally incorporated into the National Society – hence the title of a National School.

In 1843 between 50 and 60 children were 'collected' in a barn which served as their school and curate William Brooke Stevens made it clear that 'with the arrival of the harvest, they were forced to vacate their temporary home and not being able to obtain another room, it was proposed ... to build a schoolroom'.

So it was that, aided by various grants, the National School was completed at a cost of £175 on a site which was the 'free gift of Mr. Thomas Gurney of Stoke Mandeville'. The parish room now stands on this site. This gentleman farmer owned Whitethorne House (which is now the *Belmore Hotel*) and was a generous benefactor to the village; some years later, he gave an adjacent site for the building of the vicarage.

All these facts are written on the flyleaf of the Register of Baptisms together with other details. 'Seventy seven children were on the occasion regaled with beef and plum pudding and a glass of home made wine and cake in the evening ... The Master receives £13 per annum and each child pays one penny per week'. School fees were not to be abolished until 1891.

As a church school, its activities were closely monitored by the vicar who was joint trustee as well as chairman of the board of management and this led no doubt to friction with many parents within the village who were not Anglicans. As will be seen in a later chapter, there were active Primitive and Wesleyan Methodist churches established in Stoke.

10. The National School Room.

There can be no doubt that one of the aims of the far reaching Education Act of 1870 was to diminish the influence of the Anglican Church over its non-conforming parishioners. The Act laid down, amongst other things, standards of accommodation and teaching but, where the existing church schools met these requirements, they qualified for government help. Certainly at Stoke Mandeville, after initial confusion over the accommodation required for the number of children involved, the school was brought up to standard and, in 1876, Vicar Hanson reported: '... opened under Emily Anne Taylor ... newly whitewashed ... painted inside ... classroom attended to and new desks ordered'. And government funding was awaited with confidence.

A few of the teachers' names are known from directories and census records, although there are very few personal details available as no such records survive from the National School days. Some who, served were Mrs. Frances Higgins (1864), Mrs. Louisa Parsons (1869) and Mrs. King (1876).One exception, however, is Mrs. Elizabeth Langston. A directory of 1853 shows her and her class of 20 boys and 12 girls. Formerly Miss Hopcraft, she had married, in 1847, a local labourer, William Langston but probably had had very little formal training as a teacher for, upon her marriage, she was described as a servant. It seems that her husband was for many years a Sunday school teacher in spite of his lowly calling, and this is borne out by an entry in a family Bible still in the possession of a direct descendant. The inscription runs: 'Wm Langston as a reward for the excellent way in which he managed the children of the Stoke Mandeville Church Sunday School for the space of 15 years. From his Friend and fellow Teacher. T. Gurney Junr. Oct. 18th 1857'.

In the census of 1861, Mrs. Langston is found living in the Old Parsonage House in Blesbury (now Marsh) Lane which had been vacated by the vicar, Charles Partington, the same year as the new vicarage had been built in Risborough Road. The Parsonage House stood on the opposite side of the road from Silverbrook, close to the present site of the allotments. In fact, within living memory a well, thought to have belonged to the house, was found on this site.

An interesting description of the Old Parsonage was given by Mr. Partington at the opening of the new church in 1866. At the celebratory luncheon, in responding to the toast 'Drink three times three to the vicar and churchwardens of Stoke Mandeville', he recalled his early days in the village and said (although some complained they had great difficulty in hearing what he was saying after so many toasts of 'three times three'): 'In the house I first lived in, the walls were in such a state that I could without difficulty push my arm through the plaster, and, after a heavy rain, the damp was very injurious to health'. Fortunately for Mr. Partington and with the help of a benefactor, the new vicarage was built. It seems that the old one was good enough for the schoolmistress and her labourer husband. Mrs. Langston died the year after the census was taken at the age of fifty-five. Werethe selfsame damp conditions a contributory factor?

The Old Parsonage was demolished in the 1880s and was last mentioned in December 1882 by the vicar when, writing to the Local Government Board at Westminster on the matter of building a new house for the schoolmaster nearer the school, he said: 'There is but one small cottage available ... a mile or so from the school and the road to and from it is extremely bad and during the rainy season or when a fall of snow happens in winter, literally almost impassable'.

The new vicar had arrived in 1879 – the third in eight years – and Dr. Meyer Mensor could hardly be said to be an ideal incumbent for this, as it was then, desperately poor place. His gross income, which in 1880 was £180, of which £43 came from the corn rent, was well below the average stipend of the day, but, in spite of this apparent poverty, in his earlier days he was quite generous to the poorer village folk. This will be dealt with in more detail elsewhere.

In his determination to retain the National School under his control, Dr. Mensor opposed all efforts to establish a Board School under the 1870 Act.

(Board Schools became Council Schools in 1902.) The problems of the school were considerable for only a poor salary could be offered to any prospective master and this was often met, at least initially, out of the parson's own pocket. This in turn meant the post was often unfilled and the school had to be closed. With its closure the school ceased to be deemed efficient under the Act and the grant was terminated. This problem was solved in other places by rich patrons but Stoke Mandeville was without a substantial lord of the manor whose support could have eased matters.

Another problem associated with retaining a schoolmaster was the lack of suitable accommodation for, as has been seen, the Old Parsonage House was not acceptable. Plans were afoot in 1881 to build a house for the master financed partly from a National Society grant, and partly by subscription, although it is clear that the latter source came to nothing and Mensor had to pay the shortfall out of his own purse.

The proposed site for the house was the old Parish House which stood opposite the vicarage and was 'dilapidated and can be inhabited no more nor repaired and it is standing empty and going into ruins'. From written evidence given to the Local Government Board by Emanuel Edwards, the parish overseer, who had made enquiries from a previous occupier and ascertained that she had paid rent to the parish for the old cottage, it was clear that the building had been in the church's hands since the early 1840s. Before this date 'a schoolmaster lived in part of it and used the other part for a day school'. This could well have been a reference to the plaiting school which is known to have existed in the village. Information is sketchy, but in 1871 the census records a Mrs. Sarah Dixon teaching this trade and in a return showing the number of plaiting schools in the country, *The Commission of Employment of Children, Young People and Women 1867-8*, Stoke Mandeville was credited with one.

With ownership of the site no longer in question, the master's house was erected. It remains to this day on the Risborough Road as a private house called Ivy Lea (no. 49) although it has been much altered over the years. But the problems still remained. Dr. Mensor does not seem to have been the easiest person to get on with. Apart from anything else, the villagers had great difficulty in understanding his thick Germanic accent, and in turn the broad speech of the Buckinghamshire folk must have been a problem for him. He also clashed with the schoolmasters who came and went with increasing regularity.

John H. Davey held the post in 1881 and James Rose from about 1883-6. Then came a Mr. Pengelly who was there for a couple of years but was evicted from his house after Mensor dismissed him. In a long letter of 10 October 1890, addressed to the Department of Education, Mensor detailed his side of the story with a history of events. William Marsh came next but when Mensor told him he (Mensor) could no longer be responsible for paying the master's salary, Marsh resigned and the school closed again. Alfred Cox, a third certificated teacher who had been out of work for six years and whose capabilities were described as 'middling', was appointed in 1889 at a salary of £40 per annum and half of the government grant. Once again sparks began to fly when Mensor tried to exercise what he saw as his authority over the master. In his letter to the department, Mensor recalled a visit by him to the school when Cox 'in the presence of all the class said, "I shall do what I like. You have nothing to do with the school. Begone! Begone!" He then commenced clapping his hands together and afterwards danced about the school. I said, "Mr Cox, you will have to take notice to leave", and he called out, "You are not my employer" '. To add insult to injury, Mensor was also told that the children had received no religious instruction in the past school year which was contrary to the foundation deed. This was all reported to the Bishop of Reading who summoned Cox to appear before him but he sent back the answer, 'I will not come. I acknowledge no-one'.

In the middle of all this was Her Majesty's Inspector of Schools, Mr. E. M. Kenney-Herbert who, in an internal memorandum which he never thought would be read other than within the department and certainly not a hundred years later, commented, 'More trouble at this wretched place. I really do not know what is to be done'. For he himself had been involved in a bitter argument with Cox at the school. The inspector had arrived unannounced at about 3.30 in the afternoon just as the master was closing the class and Kenney-Herbert immediately opened the windows for 'the atmosphere of the room was positively awful ... I could hardly breathe in it'. Cox objected strongly to what he saw as high-handedness, saying that the school was closed and an inspection could only be entertained during school hours. Upon being told his watch was a quarter of an hour fast, Cox replied, 'I am not forced to keep Greenwich Time'. It is an interesting fact that until Railway Time, or Greenwich Time as it became known, was introduced, there were minor time variations throughout the country and the further west one went, the greater the discrepancy, although Stoke was certainly not 15 minutes adrift from Greenwich. But old habits die hard in the country.

The school was opened as a temporary measure in July 1891, under W. J. Price, who lasted a mere three months. He was followed by George Reynolds and then George T. Vickers of Little Bythan, Grantham. It was closed for a year between 1892-3 and Mr. Kenney-Herbert was of the opinion that 'Nothing has been done and I do not think that there is the slightest chance of anything being done except under compulsion. It is desirable that a School Board be set up at once as the school is certainly under Dr. Mensor's control and he shows no intention of opening it'. Then in May 1893 Mensor proudly announced to the world that the school was to reopen under a fully qualified teacher, H. P. Tattersall of Newby, Clitheroe in Lancashire and the School Inspector sent his assistant to check the situation. Harry Martin's report is worth quoting in full:

I found 11 children present, two boys and nine girls, in the main room. In the small classroom there were 25 infants making a pretty good row. I went in and could see no teacher. On asking the master who taught them, he pointed to a small boy, no bigger than several of his charges. I asked the boy his age and he answered eight and in my nineth (sic). I enquired whether this assistant was also responsible for the sewing. The master said No. Sewing was not being taught at present. I asked for a pen and ink and was told there was no ink in the school nor had there been since the present teacher had been in charge though the rector had several times promised to get some. His school was grouped around the chair on the floor of the school room. The children had reading books in their hands.

Kenney-Herbert added in his report to the Department :

The re-opening in no way affects the case for a new school. The vicar ... has long been a scandal ... not to allow the Board to let it fall back into his hands ... unless the school building is made a really efficient suitable one, it will not be re-admitted on the list of schools providing efficient accommodation. It is infamously lighted ... badly ventilated ... the classroom is a very small one ... there is no cloakroom. The Board have got a site for a new school and everything is entrain ... when this man crops up again and tries to foist his miserable little barn on us.

Mr. Kenney-Herbert had had his fill of the machinations of the Rev. Dr. Mensor. Their lordships at the Department of Education approved the recommendation and the National Society in turn recognised that the battle was lost and told Mensor, 'nothing more to be done ... I hope you will be in a position to return the £15 grant ... made under the impression that the Education Department had sanctioned the re-opening of the school and I did wrong in paying it so soon'.

Probably the first and last time a question was asked in the House of Commons concerning Stoke Mandeville occurred at this time. Sir Francis S. Powell, member of Parliament for Wigan, put down a question (no. 28) on 31 July 1893 to the Vice President of the Committee of Council on Education asking whether he was prepared to state the grounds on which he refused to allow the managers of the National School at Stoke Mandeville to reopen the school upon the annual grant and whether he would reconsider his decision.

The Minister, in his reply, stated that once the School Board was formed for the purpose of supplying the deficiency, the duty of so doing devolved upon the Board by statute and the Department had no power to accept any provision other than that made by the Board. To show the nature of the supply that the Department were asked to accept, he quoted at length from the Inspector's report.

Chapter Six

The Board School – The first 25 years

Schooling in Stoke Mandeville in the last two decades of the last century was a very hit and miss affair under the auspices of the National Society, an Anglican Church organisation based at Church House, Westminster. The Education Acts defined a public elementary school as one which had been certified efficient with adequate teachers, premises, accommodation, heating, lighting, books and so on, and to qualify for any government grant had, amongst other things, to open for 400 meetings a year; a morning and afternoon marking of the register counting as two sessions.

Without adequate funding to employ a schoolmaster and buy equipment, the school at Stoke opened irregularly which meant it did not reach the required target of 400 openings and so no grant was forthcoming. This was a vicious circle which was only broken once a School Board was established, and funding soon eased as a mysterious body called the Public Works Loan Board came to the rescue.

Dr. Mensor, the vicar, who was in a position to influence what went on at the school, for in practice it was a church school, was quite adamant in his opposition to the setting up of a School Board. He undoubtedly, and no doubt correctly, thought he would lose out when a more secular regime held the reins and so he muddled on with a series of masters who came and went with increasing regularity, but in the absence of a schoolmaster the school closed. This did not escape the notice of Her Majesty's School Inspectors and the Wycombe union officials who reported: '... again closed and there is no other school accommodation in the parish'.

The first meeting of the newly convened School Board was held at the house of Mr. Alfred Rae in Stoke Mandeville on Thursday 9 February 1893 under the chairmanship of Mr. J. H. Tapping (father of the late William Tapping) and, at a meeting four days later, the clerk was instructed to seek guidance from the Local Government Board about the duties of the School Board. At the meeting in May, tenders were out for the plans for the proposed new school building although at that time no site had been agreed upon. After a vote, Mr. W. F. Taylor's bid of 10s. was accepted. One month later, not only had the plan been prepared by Mr. Taylor but it had been submitted to, and approved by, the powers that be in Whitehall. There was a slight setback when, as mentioned in the last chapter,

Dr. Mensor attempted to block the move by opening his school after a break of a year with the appointment of yet another master. But the School Inspector's devasting report on the state of things put paid to any hope of a reprieve for the National School.

The work of the new School Board was gathering momentum. Various sites in the village were looked at and an offer by Mr. Whitchurch of Sandown on the Isle of Wight to sell 60 poles of land for £60 was accepted. The Whitchurch family had been one of the leading landowners in the parish and 100 years before this date held over 230 acres.

A petition by the villagers that a portion of a field known as the Green (Malthouse Green) should be considered was put to the meeting but lost on the chairman's casting vote. Subsequently, however, the vendor refused to sign the contract for sale as the site selected by the Board was not the one he intended to sell. Finally it was agreed that 60 poles of land belonging to Lord Rothschild at the junction of the Lower Road with Marsh Lane should be purchased for £60. A pair of thatched cottages here had just burnt down. The Local Government Board also agreed that the National School should be leased until the new one was built and Dr. Mensor's rent of £12 per annum was agreed to, as was his offer of £15 per annum for the master's house.

An advertisement was placed in the *School Guardian* on 2 September 1893 for a headteacher and the successful applicant was Mr. Christopher Edward Arnold, master of the National Boys School, at Yardley Hastings, a village in Northamptonshire about three miles from Olney and three times the size of Stoke

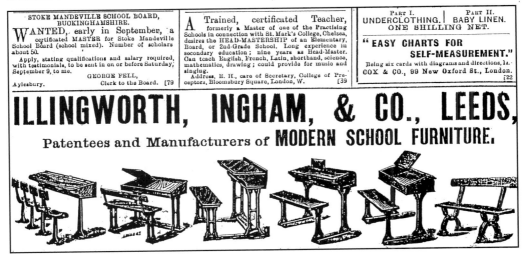

11.   Advertising for a Master for the Board School in the *School Guardian*, 2 September 1893.

Mandeville. His appointment was duly confirmed at a salary of £80 per annum, and the house, with his wife Eliza as sewing mistress. Miss Edith Mason became an assistant at a salary of £6 per annum and classes opened on 3 October 1893 in the old school. In the meantime tenders were out for the new building, and that of Mr. George Gibson of High Wycombe for £898 10s. was accepted. The work was completed and the move made in January 1895.

Mr. Arnold soon established himself as an outstanding teacher, although to begin with he found the children backward. He wrote in the school log: 'I found the older children generally in a very backward condition, and am unable to class any at present above Standard 3. The children under seven years of age are not equal to the lower class of any ordinary infant school, the majority of them hardly knowing their letters'. The Rev. Dr. Mensor's years of disorder and confusion were being felt.

Even before the school had moved to the new site, Mensor was complaining about the closets at his National School (after all they were practically at his back door!), and orders were given 'for the same to be emptied and cleansed'. Incidentally, the first cleaning lady, Mrs. Jane Eames received 1s. per week for the 46 weeks of the school year and when she asked for an increase in salary to take into account the need to empty the cesspool, the Board offered her husband £1 per annum to deal with the matter. Only two years after the new school was opened, the Sanitary Inspector was complaining about an open ditch into which the wash-houses emptied and an order was made to 'disconnect' them from the ditch. It is not clear from the log how the original problem was overcome, for it was another 50 years or so before Stoke Mandeville was connected with mains drainage.

The school's full complement of pupils was 35 (both boys and girls) and 32 infants, and children were allowed to be enrolled from adjoining parishes although overcrowding often put a stop to this arrangement. 'Outsiders' had to make room for local children. In 1906 the school log records that 'A girl from Bishopstone applied for admission to the school this morning but as the upper room is already overfull, I was obliged to refuse admission'. And again eight weeks later: '... instructions from the Bucks County Education Committee ordering the removal of children under five years of age and also the exclusion of two children from Weston Turville parish'.

It was often easier for children living in outlying areas of one parish to go to school in an adjoining one. When defining compulsory attendance, the Education Act stated that a child should not have more than two miles to travel from home and if it meant going into another parish whose school was nearer, rather than have no education at all, this was the practical answer. But the School Board often disagreed. By now, however, education had become the responsibility of the county council, as local School Boards were abolished in 1902 and schools were given the title of Council School. Perhaps the old Board would have been more sympathetic in such cases, knowing the local difficulties.

As Mr. Arnold was the only certified teacher on the premises, his absence for any reason meant the school had to be closed. 'The school kept only a short time this afternoon, to enable me to catch the 4.15 train at Aylesbury on urgent business'. But the headmaster frequently closed the school for other reasons rather than see his percentage attendance drop when he anticipated pupils were going to be absent. The annual grant depended partly upon good and regular attendance.

> A meet of foxhounds in the village today. Closed at 11.30 and re-opened at 2 to enable children to see the meet. Several of the boys followed the hunt too far and were absent this afternoon ... called up the boys who were absent yesterday afternoon and punished them all.

Mr. Arnold's success was such that within 10 years the school was bursting at the seams and, as an inspector reported in 1905, the resources and building were stretched to the utmost.

> Mr. Arnold is attempting the impossible. To try and teach effectively the whole of the upper school single handed and at the same time exercise sufficient supervision of the work of the infant class teacher is a task beyond the power of any man ... the main room is getting too small for the number of children in regular attendance, and the desk accommodation is quite insufficient.

There followed a public enquiry by the Buckinghamshire county council concerning the alleged lack of room for the older scholars but it was not until 1908 that the promised improvement was implemented and an extra classroom was added at the cost of £400. 'Closed the school at noon today, for the Whitsuntide holiday, specially extended to three weeks for building purposes'.

From time to time local outbreaks of contagious illness made their mark on the school:

> The second death of a scholar from diphtheria took place this morning; that of Emma Smith aged 10, Standard 4, her sister, Elizabeth Smith, Upper Infants having died on 28 July. The school closed this morning until the end of the month under authority of the Medical Officer of Health, on account of the epidemic of diphtheria.

The school closed in June for the hay harvest and again in August for the main harvest as most of the children of all ages were in the fields helping their parents gather in the crops.

> Re-opened the school this morning, the holidays being extended to 6 weeks on account of the protracted harvest. The attendance fell off considerably after the

early part of the week, several of the upper school being engaged in the harvest fields. Allowed some of the scholars to have school two hours after registers closed in afternoons this week to carry tea to hayfields.

Until 1918, when the school leaving age was raised to 14, education was compulsory up to 10 years of age when children could be certified by the School Inspector as having achieved Standard 5. But if pupils had registered too few attendances, they had to stay on until the age of thirteen. This could mean a potentially gifted child, who was bright enough to reach the fifth grade before 13 but was unlikely to be able to go on to further education as the family needed him or her as a breadwinner, could, and often did, leave early.

The older children were, however, being prepared for adult life in other ways. There was a girls' laundry class held at the local 'big house' of which Stoke Mandeville was notably short – big houses as well as laundries! This was undoubtedly one way of introducing the girls to the wash tub, and also enabled Stoke House to have its laundry done quite economically. The boys were otherwise engaged in handicraft classes. These were held in Aylesbury and a recommendation was made by the school managers following a suggestion that the boys could go in by train: 'The classes should be once a fortnight for the whole day instead of a half day once a week. The Managers considered that the Stoke Mandeville boys would be well able to walk both ways'.

In the days when it was not unpopular to be patriotic, national and local events featured regularly in the log.

> The Queen's birthday and the relief of Mafeking. We celebrated these events by parading the village during the afternoon about 3.30 with flags, singing the National Anthem and other patriotic songs. Returned to school about 4 o'clock. Counted as an object lesson in loyalty.
>
> Empire Day. I gave an address to the school this afternoon on the greatness of our Empire, and on the duties and responsibilities of its people, encouraging the children to do all they could to improve themselves and to be ready to take up their duties when their time came. Patriotic songs were afterwards sung, and play time slightly extended.
>
> Last part of the morning spent in playground, the children watching with interest the military aeroplanes etc. connected with the manoeuvres. Bell rang as usual for afternoon school at 2 o'clock but so small a number of children attended that I though it best to close for the day, the greater part of the village having gone to see the marching past of the troops at the Wendover turn.

The First World War seems to have affected the school greatly. Not only did Mr. Arnold, whose driving force was clearly evident from the outset, retire in 1914 while his successor, Miss Starck, remained for only a year, but numbers dropped. The remaining children's energies were directed into other channels such as collecting eggs for the sick soldiers and blackberry and chestnut gathering. The latter is quite interesting to relate. It is an example of how a plan to involve non-combatants in a war, to make them feel they were helping in some way, failed to have the desired effect. It was on a par with the plan for the collection of aluminium saucepans during the Second World War which also had no useful conclusion.

The collection of horse chestnuts had official backing, being the brainchild of the Ministry of Munitions, which claimed in 1917 that their collection would conserve the food supply. For every ton collected there would be a saving of half a ton of barley which was being used in the manufacture of T.N.T. (A spirit was extracted from the nuts as a substitute.) Schools all over the country were being urged to collect them 'as they fall' and it would seem that children in areas where horse chestnuts grew went to work with a will. Buckinghamshire's contribution was 5 per cent of the country's total of 2,200 tons, but unfortunately many children were disappointed when collection difficulties left piles of rotting nuts on railway sidings where they had been dumped.

The shortage of fuel during, and immediately after, the First World War was very severe. In a Ministry circular sent just 11 days before the Armistice was signed, economy of fuel and light in the schools was sought, and 'extravagance was to be checked'. But Stoke had long suffered from shortages and the dictate must have been received with less than enthusiasm by the headteacher:

> The supply of coal has run out and coal ordered has not come. For three days we have kept going with only two small fires of slack and cinders.
>
> I kept the children until 11 o'clock doing physical exercise – dancing and games – the coal still not having arrived ...
>
> Half a ton of coal received today; this was emptied into the road and the boys had to get it into the coal house.

It has been seen how, in the early days, the school relied on the headteacher absolutely and his absence for any reason meant that the school had to close. Any available assistants supervised the infants but seemed to have a limited role and certainly had to provide their own accommodation. One exception to this rule was, of course, Mr. Arnold's own daughters, two of whom acted in this capacity. Miss M. F. Arnold was appointed as a probationer in 1899 at a salary of £5 per annum and it is interesting to note from the manager's minute book that, when the quarterly cheque was written out for her own and her father's salary, the total sum was made out to him! Miss Arnold left the school upon her marriage in 1909 to Mr. Samuel G. Johnson but rejoined for a while on a temporary basis. Her younger sister, Miss Edith, was also taken on in 1916 after her father retired.

By the first decade of this century supply teachers seemed to be available in case of absence, but how this was actually organised is not clear. What is obvious, however, is that it was fraught with difficulties:

Mrs. A. Turner, Certified Trainee Mistress, commenced her work this morning as a supply teacher ... unable to reach the school before 12 o'clock owing to a connection taken from Oxford being late at Princes Risborough.

Miss Tuckett arrived at school today mid-day to assist as Supplementary Teacher in the upper room ... seized with an illness this morning and quite unable to attend school ... Miss Tuckett left for home today, Bampton Aston, Oxon. being unable to continue her work.

12. Mr. and Mrs. Arnold with their grandchildren in the garden of Bushey Cottage, c.1921.

On such occasions the timetable had to be rearranged accordingly, for even the doughty Arnold was not willing to teach the girls their sewing: 'Drawing substituted for needlework with girls this afternoon in absence of teacher for needlework'. The position of monitoress was also a paid one but her duties were again restricted to the infants. Even the older children were sometimes co-opted to help in this area; 'the elder children take the five younger infants in turn'.

Christopher Arnold retired from duty in 1914 after 43 years in the teaching profession, 20 of them at Stoke Mandeville. The visiting School Inspector commented upon his 'straight forward devotion to duty in this little village

13. Standards I, II and III in 1931. First row, from left: Jessie Spence, Rene Kidnee, Peggy Ward; second row: Betty Webb, Ruby Montague, Margaret Ballard, Arthur Cutler, Dennis Cheshire; third row: Freda Smith, Margaret Robson, Gwen Edmunds, ?, Ronald Webb, Ronald Allen; fourth row: Sheila Irving, John Leader, Maurice King, Peter Starling, Philip Leader, Kitty Burrell; fifth row: Ted Haily, Cedric Miles, Robert White, Alec Bailey.

14. Standards IV, V and VI in 1931. First row, from left: Winnie Bates, Phyllis Thatcher, Dorothy Ward, Peggy Leader; second row: Ted Hayers, Ron Welford, Betty Smith, Phyllis Irvine; third row: Charles Kidnee, Jim Purssell, Charles Spence, Kathleen Webb, Harry Allen; fourth row: Joan White, Patsy Kershaw, George Irvine; back row: Lily Edmonds, Peggy Wiggins, Douglas Brooke, Bill Budd.

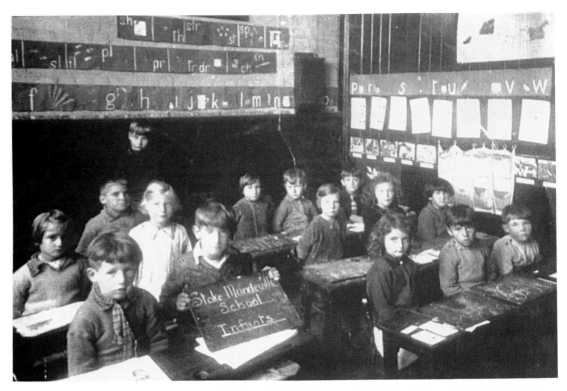

15. Infants class in 1931. First row, from left: Laurie Webb, Raymond Munday, Norma White, Frank Cutler, Arthur Cheshire; second row: Doreen Miles, Audrey Webb, Peggy Cheshire, Irene Sheriff, Lucy Purssell; third row: Francis White, Peggy Miles, Tom Spencer, Frank Watson; fourth row: ?.

16. The school in 1948. Back row, from left: A. Mead, J. Lake, C. Middleton, M. Purssell, M. Collins, Mr. A. Green; middle row: S. Allen, D. Woodend, M. Atkins, J. Morgan, D. Luxton, N. Weatherhead; front row: D. Chapple, A. Putnam, M. Curtis, L. Burgin, R. Pratt, M. Storr, M. Webb.

community', adding that 'his presence and kindly influence will be greatly missed'. These words proved prophetic for, almost inevitably, he proved impossible to follow, especially as he continued to live in the village with his family at the New House, Moat Farm.

Whilst there is no suggestion or indeed evidence of any kind that he interfered with, or tried to influence the work of his successor, it is a fact that Miss Jane Alice Starck from Ashendon lasted a mere 12 months. Mr. Arnold was called back for a short while pending the appointment of Miss F. M. P. Taylor of Silesby near Loughborough. She was at the school during the worst part of the First World War when the trauma and carnage was at its height, and her resignation in 1919 brought the school's first 25 years to a close.

What had been achieved in those two and a half decades of the board school? Thanks to the work and professionalism of all concerned, an isolated and relatively backward village community had been brought, through the devotion to its children, quietly and steadily into the 20th century.

17.   The school football team, 1948-9. Back row, from left: N. Weatherhead, D. Luxton, D. Woodend, J. Morgan, K. O'Brien, M. Atkins, I. Jones, J. Goulbourn; front row: R. Rowell, B. Ward, S. Allen, D. Chapple, T. Earwicker.

Additional classrooms were added in 1956 at cost of about £7,000 when nearly an acre of the allotments was sold to the county council for £1,200. The builders were Messrs. A. & G. Simmons of Wendover. Another one and a half acres were sold in 1972 for further extensions. On this occasion, however, thanks to an astute move by the parish council, the price obtained for the land was based on that for building rather than agricultural purposes as had happened in 1956. The bulk of this windfall, which was in the region of £100,000, was utilised in the building of the Community Centre.

Although it is too early to give a balanced or objective view of subsequent events, particularly as many of the people are still alive, a history of the school would be incomplete without mention of subsequent headteachers at least by name.

Miss Olive Mole served the school from 1919-44, five years longer than Mr. Arnold's own tenure, and this period included the aftermath of the First World War, the depression of the '30s, a further contraction of the village population and finally into another World War. She is remembered with affection and respect by many who passed through the school as indeed is Mr. Alfred Green who was headteacher from 1948-68, who still lives in the area, and Mrs. J. Last who followed him until her early retirement in 1984. At the time of writing the present headteacher is Mr. John Ainsworth, and the school's current designation is Stoke Mandeville County Combined.

Chapter Seven

The Methodist Church

There has been a Methodist church in Stoke Mandeville since the early years of the movement although, at first, the meetings would probably have been held in the room of a cottage or in a barn. It seems inconceivable that it is only since civil registration just over 150 years ago that a marriage other than in an Anglican church was legally enforceable in law, apart from Jewish and Quaker marriages, which were exempt from the provisions of the Hardwicke Act of 1753 and subsequent legislation.

Although it is clear that Roman Catholics had their secret places and Nonconformists continued to marry in their local chapels, this was often laying up trouble for their children in any subsequent dispute. On such occasions everyone bar the chapel cat signed the register as witnesses. The more who were available to testify in later years to the happy event the better.

Until civil registration changed all this, meeting houses had to be registered with the justices, and the names of the occupiers of the premises which appear in the various Quarter Session records for Stoke Mandeville were: 1765, Benjamin Goodspeed; 1774, John Atkins; 1811, William Mead; 1824, William Ayres; and 1839, Henry Allen.

That in the house of William Mead is positively identified as Methodist, but with the others neither the denomination nor venue is known, and indeed one or more undoubtedly referred to Prestwood Common where there was a very strong Baptist following. Thomas Ford Jnr., a blacksmith, made it clear in his appeal against the enclosure commissioner's allotment that his premises on Lower Road, which had previously been used as a chapel, had been converted into tenements. So whatever little place of worship might have been there, it no longer existed in 1797.

As recently as 1926, one of the five cottages which stood on the east side of the Risborough Road (now Burgoyne and Spencer Cottages) beyond the *Woolpack Inn* went by the name of Chapel Row, and, as mentioned elsewhere, the same property is described in 1910 in a sale catalogue map of Stoke House Farm, as a Methodist chapel.

The Wesleyan Methodist chapel, on the corner of Chapel Lane and Risborough Road, was rebuilt there in 1868 at a cost of £180, close to or on the site of an earlier building of 1815. The foundation stone of the new building was laid

18. The Methodist chapel, built in 1868.   19. Interior of the Methodist chapel.

on 9 July by Mr. Thomas Twitchell of Bedford. £5 was paid for the original piece of land which measured 24 ft. wide and 30 ft. long, and was formerly part of the yard of William Fleet's carpenter shop. The building itself cost about £120 in 1815. Was the earlier place of worship on the other side of the road or was it only housed there during the rebuilding? Perhaps it was used by a different denomination altogether or perhaps the map itself was at fault.

It must have been a struggle for the Methodist community, and at times, particularly when the only form of poor relief came out of parish rates, it was a hard decision to remain faithful to the chapel when being pressurised by the overseer of the poor of the parish to conform. Religious pressure eased somewhat, however, after the 1834 Act of Parliament which took the direct responsibility for relief out of the parish's hands into the larger unit of the Guardian of the Poor via the Union Workhouse.

When in 1851 the Places of Religious Worship return was taken, the census for the Wesleyans showed an average attendance of 80 at each of the afternoon and evening services as well as a Sunday school of 21. On the day of the return 70 were there in the afternoon, 75 in the morning and 14 at Sunday school. Reuben Smith signed as steward. There was free seating for 80 and 48 other places. At the Primitive Methodists, probably in the dwelling place of William Tapping who signed the return as class leader, there was no Sunday school, while 25 attended in the morning and 24 in the evening. There was room for 40 free seatings. The Anglican church failed to make a return.

It is interesting to note some of the comments made. The Anglicans were positively hostile to the operation and either did not respond, as at Stoke Mandeville, or either accused their Nonconforming neighbours of inflating the attendance figures for their own devious means, or blamed their own low numbers on the weather. It was yet another example of 'them and us', now happily a thing of the past.

The chapel had to be financially self supporting. The minister or circuit preacher did not have the corn rent or tithes to fall back upon to supplement his income, and the chapel dues had to be found out of the pennies and half-pennies of the faithful.

There is an account book, recently deposited in the county archives, which reveals how hand to mouth things were at times. In 1910 the seat rents were £1 per annum. Cleaning cost 5s. per quarter and fire insurance was 3s. 9d. per annum. But everyone seems to have rallied round when funds were wanted. The proceeds of a lecture raised 13s. 6d. and the 1915 Harvest Festival and sale £4 6s. 6d.– a not inconsiderable sum for those days.

As the Second World War drew to a close and most young people started to return to civilian life, there was only a handful of worshippers left at the Stoke Mandeville chapel. One member tells the story of the chapel harmonium. It had done sterling work for many years but its bellows were patched and it creaked and wheezed as if terminally ill. Something had to be done.

She and the chapel organist set out to Mr. Rose's workshop in the Bicester Road to seek a replacement. Whilst the organist played away to her heart's content on one of the organs on the premises, Mr. Rose asked her companion how much they could afford to spend and was told £18, the proceeds of a recent sale of work. Seemingly the organist had set her heart on the instrument on which she had been playing so merrily. 'It's a beautiful organ but I doubt we shall be able to afford it. How much are you asking?', to which the benevolent Mr. Rose replied, I'll take £18'. (His sister, Mrs Richardson, lived at nearby St Mary's Cottage for many years.) This American organ was taken into the new church in due course and gave full value for many years.

By 1950, however, it was clear that the church at the corner of Chapel Lane and Risborough Road, which had served the community for 150 years, had become overcrowded and outmoded. The decision was made, as the existing building could not be enlarged, to seek new premises for the growing membership. It was eight years' hard work of fund raising before a target of £8,000 was reached and work could start.

A site had been found in Eskdale Road and on Saturday 24 May 1958 the stone-laying ceremony and dedication took place. The stone was laid by Mrs. H. M. Dennis, widow of a former Aylesbury Circuit superintendent and the

20. The opening of the new Methodist chapel in 1958.

21. Methodist church Christmas Party 1971. Back row, from left: Mrs. Marshall, ? Tye, Y. Lane, ? Tye; front row: M. Lane, I. Chapman, P. Vernon, A. Garter, A. Chapman.

dedication made by the Rev. L. O. Brooker, chairman of the North-West District. The Aylesbury Methodist Circuit minister and the ministers of both Whitchurch and Stoke Mandeville churches were also present. Afterwards tea was taken in the Ex-Servicemen's Hall. As the newspaper report at the time commented:

> The new, contemporary-style, church was opened on Saturday [25 October 1958] by Mrs. L. O. Brooker, the wife of the chairman of the North-West District. The building contains a dual-purpose hall in which services are held. It is fitted with a steel curtain which enables the communion table to be separated from the rest of the hall which can then be used for social activities. Gifts too numerous to list were given to the church by various members.

Chapter Eight

Inclosure, thou'rt a curse upon the land and tasteless was the wretch who thy existence plann'd

Enclosure of the land, which took place over hundreds of years, was either a good thing or a bad one according to one's situation and station in life. The above couplet by John Clare, the village poet of Helpston in Northamptonshire, shows clearly where he stood.

In Elizabethan times the Crown tried to discourage and prohibit enclosures to preserve a more equitable society, but as time went by the landowning classes, who on the whole dominated Parliament and the justices and later on the higher enclaves of what was to become local government, had no such scruples and adopted a less patriarchal attitude. The landowners and larger farmers, who could afford the cost of enclosure, gained a more easily worked and administered property which often doubled in value, whilst the cottager and smallholder frequently lost parts of their acreage for new roads and as recompense to the titheholder for loss of dues.

When the enclosure for Stoke Mandeville took place, the Dean and Chapter of Lincoln and their Lessees, the Governors of Christ's Hospital, were allocated over 25 acres of meadow land in the north of the parish towards Stone for loss of tithes and glebe, and Lord Grenville gained 24 acres adjoining his existing land in the West Field for surrendering vicarial tithes. This provided a viable 170-acre holding. Similarly the lord of the manor was allocated 79 acres of the Rivey Field which had earlier formed part of the wide band of common land east of the Lower Road near his own Manor Farm. Lord Hampden up in Prestwood, however, did less well and his existing 120 acres were merely noted as part of an earlier enclosure.

Compensation to labourers for loss of rights was sometimes provided and this included the allocation of garden allotments. The idea was that cultivation of such plots would help out with fresh vegetables for the family and the additional interest engendered would act as a counter attraction to the ale-house. Such plots were provided just outside the parish boundary in a 40-acre field called Bradleys, south of Marsh Lane, opposite the entrance to Apsley Farm. A subsequent owner was Lord Rothschild, who also held Brook Farm, and in his time these allotments were transferred to another site of his nearer the village.

The poor villager, whose traditional access to the common land for the grazing of a sheep or cow was an essential part of life, was a casualty when the

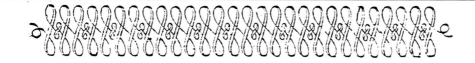

AN

A C T

FOR

Dividing and Inclosing the Open and Common Fields, Common Meadows, and other Commonable Lands, within the Parish of *Stoke Mandeville*, in the County of *Buckingham*.

WHEREAS there are within the Parish of *Stoke Mande-* Preamble. *ville*, in the County of *Buckingham*, certain Open and Common Fields, Common Meadows, and other Commonable Lands, containing One Thousand Acres, or thereabouts, and divers Quantities of Meadow and Pasture Land:

And whereas the Dean and Chapter of the Cathedral Church of the Blessed Virgin *Mary* of *Lincoln*, are Patrons of the Vicarage of *Bierton*, in the said County of *Buckingham*, with the Vicarage or Chapelry of *Stoke Mandeville* aforesaid thereto annexed, and are also seised of the Appropriate Rectory of *Stoke Mandeville* aforesaid, consisting of certain Glebe Lands lying in the said Open and Common Fields, Common Meadows, and Commonable Lands, in the Parish of *Stoke Mandeville* aforesaid, together with the Great or Appropriate Tythes Yearly arising and renewing within the said Parish of *Stoke Mandeville*, or to certain Payments or Compositions in lieu thereof respectively:

And whereas the Mayor and Commonalty, and Citizens of the City of *London*, Governors of the Possessions, Revenues, and Goods

A

of

22. The Act of Parliament for enclosing the parish, 1798.

commons were enclosed, and this was certainly so in Stoke Mandeville. Very early maps of the area show a wide band of common land either side of the road leading from Aylesbury to Stoke Mandeville and down towards Terrick. This was swept away when enclosure took place.

Over 1,000 acres were enclosed and the schedule of properties contained 59 names and 195 individual allotments of land, homesteads, cottages and orchards, together with 'several roads', with an area in excess of 28 acres and an allotment to the Surveyors of the Highway of the parish. There was also a field of three quarters of an acre on the west side of the Lower Road, near the

And be it further Enacted, That the said Commissioners shall, **Roads to be** and they are hereby required, in the First Place, to set out and **set out.** appoint such public Roads and Highways to, through, and over the Lands and Grounds hereby intended to be divided and inclosed, as they in their Discretion shall think requisite, the public Carriage and Drift Roads to be and remain of the Breadth of Forty Feet at least in every Part thereof between the Ditches or Fences, and shall be well and sufficiently fenced on both Sides, by such of the Owners and Proprietors of the said Lands and Grounds hereby intended to be divided and inclosed, and within such Time as the said Commissioners shall, by any Writing under their Hands, direct or appoint; and that it shall not be lawful for any Person or Persons to set up or erect a Gate across any such public Carriage or Drift Roads, or to plant any Trees in or near to the Hedges on the Sides thereof at a less Distance from each other than Fifty Yards; and that after the said public Carriage Roads shall have been set out as hereinbefore is directed, the said Commissioners shall, and they **Surveyor to** are hereby required, by Writing under their Hands, to appoint **be appoint-** some proper Person to be Surveyor thereof, who shall cause the **ed.** same to be formed and put into good State and Condition; and such Surveyor shall be allowed such Salary for his Trouble therein as the said Commissioners shall, by Writing under their Hands, order and direct; which Salary, and also the Expence of forming the said public Roads, and putting the same into good State and Condition (over and above the Statute Duty) shall be raised in like Manner as the Charges and Expences of obtaining and passing this Act, and of carrying the same into Execution, are hereinafter directed to be raised, so as that none of the Inhabitants of the Parish of *Stoke Mandeville* aforesaid, other than the Owners and Proprietors for the Time being of the Lands and Grounds hereby intended to be divided,

                                        C

23. Setting-out of public roads and highways under the Act.

present Buckinghamshire County Staff Sports and Social Club, which the Commissioners allocated to the Trustees for Stoke Poor. When let, its rent was earmarked solely for buying fuel for village poor and was the Annabella Ligo Charity land. This was sold for £100 in 1929 to Edward Brown, who was a dairyman living nearby at Silver Leet.

The act also laid down clear guidelines to the Commissioners for its implementation. No lambs were to be kept in the new enclosures for four years and all allotments were to be fenced before execution of the award. Landowners were sent bills for the fencing and many smallholders were unable to meet the cost. Damaging this fencing was a prosecution matter.

Ten years or so later, in 1810, the Rev. St. John Priest, writing in *A General View of the Agriculture of Buckinghamshire*, viewed the after-effects of the act on the village and gave details. Of the enclosure, arable of 700 acres was by far the largest part, followed by 220 acres of pasture, 110 acres of meadow and a mere 20 acres of woodland mostly at Prestwood. There were 10 farmhouses where the land under cultivation varied between 20 to 600 acres and 10 cottages, although there were many other 'Hovels and Tenements', too insignificant to list. This is shown by the census taken four years later when there were said to be 80 houses

---

And be it further Enacted, That it shall and may be lawful to and for the said Commissioners, and they are hereby authorized and required (if they shall think it necessary and proper) to set out and appoint, out of and from the Lands and Grounds hereby intended to be divided and inclosed, One or more Piece or Pieces of Ground, not exceeding Five Acres, for the Purpose of getting Materials for repairing the Roads and Ways already made, or to be set out by virtue of this Act, and for such other Uses as the said Commissioners shall direct; and that the Herbage growing and renewing in and upon the said Piece or Pieces of Ground, shall be vested in such Person or Persons as the said Commissioners, in and by their Award, shall order and direct. *Stone and Gravel Pits.*

---

24.   Allocation of stone and gravel pits under the Act.

in the parish. The actual effect of the enclosure was to decrease the number of sheep and pigs held and the volume of wheat, barley and beans also decreased by a third.

The act relating to Stoke Mandeville, passed by Parliament in 1797, appointed the Commissioners. These were the Rev. Joseph Smith of Wendover, John Fellows gent. of Westcott and Edward Platt gent. of Lidlington, Bedfordshire. They met for the first time at the *George* in Aylesbury on Friday 23 June

1797 and immediately suspended, until further notice, all rights of common for sheep and cattle in open and common fields. They then required all occupiers of common land to attend the duly appointed surveyors in setting out 'Common Ground, Jointways, Headlands and Furlongs'. The owners and occupiers had to mark their land and leys at both ends as to tenure, that is freehold or copyhold, and finally had to provide two or more labourers to attend in the valuation. The owners then had to give, in writing, details of every piece of land on which they had an interest. As has been seen, there were winners and losers when the final allotments were established but those who appealed did not get very far with the Commissioners. It is fortunate that the original notebooks and minutes of the various meetings and appeals still survive in the county archives.

Whilst it is impossible to go into every case in detail, one in particular is now examined to show how the act worked. In his deposition, the Rev. Charles Garden of Pangbourne listed all his holdings in the common fields which had been acquired upon his marriage to the widow Maria Mead. Incidentally the word land or sellion used in this context has been defined as 'a cultivated strip in a open field consisting of a ridge with a furrow on either side'. The names of owners of the adjoining lands have been omitted for the sake of brevity but his holdings consisted of:

> One acre in the Rivey Field, otherwise Middle Field. Half an acre in a furlong called Sutton's Hill, the lands of ... and Downway on the east end. Half an acre more in the same field, Long Cross Furlong ... and shooting into gores upon a Ley late of ... Half an acre in the Mead Field at Great Butts, shooting on the headland. One acre lying together in ditto in Mead Furlong abutting upon old bridge on the west. One acre in the Causeway Field in Trunk Furlong ... one land abutting on the Causeway east. Two acres more in the same field in a place called Walling; three lands lie together in Causeway Furlong ... the Causeway the east end, through other land in Walling in the Butt Furlong ... abutting to Pond Mead on the west and abutting to one of the three lands of ... One acre and a half more in the same field in Causeway Furlong, two lands near together only one land ... lying between them. The other land in the Causeway field in a furlong called Smallthorne Lane ... one wood in a field called Benhill or Bennell ... and a common way called Reeds Lane. One half acre in the aforesaid Mead Field in new Hitchin ... the house ground on the north. Two acres in Halend piece, three lands lying together in a furlong called Chapel furlong ... abutting on Long Crossway east ... the other lands lyeth further northwards ... Long Crossway furlong. One land and one rood lying in Long Cross furlong the said land lieth between ... lands abutting on Long Crossway and the said rood lieth further northwards ... and abutteth on Long Crossway ... containing together eleven and a half acres all freehold.

Mr. Garden's 11 pieces of scattered land, some as small as one perch, were reduced to just under eight acres in one lot when the allocation was made. Upon Maria's death, Mr. Garden alienated the property to John Gurney. From just this one example can be seen the problems the Commissioners were up against and it is little wonder that unfair decisions appear to have been made.

The corn rent formed an important part of the income of clergymen, and at Stoke Mandeville in the 1880s it represented a quarter of the incumbent's benefice of £180 per annum. This local levy was introduced at the time of the enclosures in lieu of vicarial tithes and the rent was based on the average price of a 'Winchester Bushel of good marketable wheat within the County of Buckinghamshire'. There was then a complicated calculation based on the yield per acre to arrive at the charge and a revision based upon the current value of wheat took place every seven or 14 years.

| Compensa-tion for Vi-carial Tythes. | And, in order to make Compensation to the Vicar of the said Parish of *Stoke Mandeville* aforesaid, in lieu of all his Vicarial or Small Tythes, which are intended to be extinguished by virtue of this Act, Be it further Enacted, That the said Commissioners shall, and they are hereby authorized and required, in the first Place, to make or cause to be made distinct or separate Estimates of the Annual Value of such of the Lands and Grounds hereby intended to be divided and inclosed, and of such of the Homesteads, Orchards, Gardens, and Home Closes, within the said Parish of *Stoke Mandeville*, as are subject to the Payment of Vicarial or Small Tythes, or to any Composition in lieu thereof; and the said Commissioners shall, from and by Means of the *London Gazette*, and by such other Ways and Means as they shall think most proper, enquire what hath been the Average Price of a *Winchester* Bushel of good Marketable Wheat in the County of *Buckingham* during the Term of Fourteen Years next |

25. Establishment of the corn rent at Stoke Mandeville.

In 1797 the price was said to be 6s. 3d. per bushel and had risen to 7s. 3d. by 1841. In that year the Parish House on the Risborough Road, referred to elsewhere, was assessed at 3¼d. per annum. As the price of wheat rose over the years, so did the rent alongside it and, as time went by, landowners began to try to redeem the charge on their properties in the same way as tithes.

About 170 acres were redeemed in 1898 when there were both rectorial and vicarial rents in force. The redemption figure was between 25 and 30 times the annual rent but the local clergy did not benefit directly for it was paid to the Governors of Queen Anne's Bounty – the forerunner of the Church Commissioners for England, the body dealing with Church revenues. The process was repeated in 1902, 1924 and 1949. The smallest piece of land dealt with in this manner was 'In the Hook' towards Hartwell, a little over half an acre, on which an annual rental of 1¼d. was redeemed for 3s. 1¼d.

The Lords of the Manor

The position of lord of the manor has existed since medieval times but, as mentioned elsewhere, Stoke Mandeville has never, in recent times, had a wealthy owner who could carry out traditional activities associated with the landed gentry including the establishment and funding of a school. Since the end of the 18th century, holders have been little more than prosperous farmers at the Manor Farm.

The Stoke Mandeville Court Book from 1786 to 1867 has recently come to light and has been deposited in the county archives by the Aylesbury solicitors, Messrs. Parrott & Coles. One of the partners acted as steward of the manor in the last century and the book had been retained in their archives until its deposit. This is of great interest as it covers the period of the village's history from just before the enclosure act to halfway through the last century. A detailed study of this book would uncover many interesting facts which have lain hidden for many years and would be particularly helpful in identifying some of the old field names.

The court met irregularly, every five to 20 years, and when it sat a jury of 12 men, after acknowledging their allegiance to the lord or lady in an act of frankpledge, went on to inform the court, from their personal knowledge of local affairs, what had happened in the intervening years. In the period before enclosure, clear guidelines were laid down:

> **1786** ... ordered that no sheep be turned on the clover in the bean field after old Candlemas Day yearly until the expiration of 21 days after all the corn and grain is cleared and if any sheep shall be found therein between the above times, the Hayward or Fields Men shall be at liberty to impound them til the owner or owners of such sheep shall pay the Pinlock ... also ordered that no great cattle shall be suffered to go into the Common Meadow after the twenty fifth day of December yearly til all the hay be cleared upon like penalty.

Property transactions were described and new ownerships established either by inheritance or alienation:

> **1806** From Luke Berry to Thomas Berry, at a yearly rent of 3s. 9d., a cottage called the Wool Pack.
> **1806** From Thomas Fleet who held freely from the Lord of the Manor by fealty suit of Court and yearly rental of 3d. on a cottage and garden of 29 perches now known by the sign of the *Bull* to Richard Terry.

Encroachments upon the waste were also reported and a suitable amerceation (fine) agreed upon.

> **1806** John Smith of the Pigeon House hath made an encroachment upon the waste by enclosing part of the road near his cottage by the *Bull* public house.

Ordered to throw open within three calendar months under penalty of 6d. per annum until same is thrown open.

1806 James Fleet hath set up a sign post for the present *Bull* public house upon the waste of this Manor which is an encroachment thereon wherefore the said James Fleet is amerced for the same 1d. and is ordered to remove the same within three calendar months under penalty of 1d. so long as the same shall continue.

1806 Toby Impey hath encroached upon the waste by enclosing a piece of the road in front of the *Bull* public house and converted same into a garden wherefore the said Toby Impey is amerced 6d. and ordered to throw open the same and pay 6d. per annum until the same is thrown open.

In spite of this, Impey was appointed constable of the parish the same year, so incroachments do not seem to have been taken too seriously. Provided the fine was paid they continued year after year, and even the Church authorities were not guiltless:

1819 Churchwardens and Overseers of the Poor made an encroachment on the waste of this Manor by erecting four cottages and enclosing the ground adjoining the Manor Farm wherefore they are amerced for the sum of 5s. and the same per annum to the Lord so long as such encroachment shall continue.

The court appointed the officers of the manor and these included the constable, fields men and hay ward. Finally, recommendations were made on general matters:

1806 ... the stocks belonging to this Court are out of repair and the same ought to be repaired at the expense of the Lord of the Manor ... also presented by the Jury that there is not a Pound within this Manor and a convenient Pound ought to be build or provided by the Lord of the Manor. [At Walton, in the adjoining parish, the stables of the *Old Plough and Harrow Inn* were at one time used as a village pound.]

The last lord of the manor, John Henry Tapping, died in 1921 and left all his properties in trust for his family; these in turn were sold at auction in 1945. It would be interesting to know whether the lordship was sold at the same time.

Chapter Nine

Parish Services

We've had the proper water fitted on – Council water in pipes. I don't care for it myself,
don't seem to be no strength in it.
You can't hardly taste it, can't even smell it.
Give me a drop of my old well water anytime.
You can smell that alright. That's why they made me fill it in.

The late Sir Bernard Miles's *One of the Old School.*

Until 100 years ago, the village was completely dependent on its wells for drinking water and every cottage had its water butt to augment supplies for washing and other less essential purposes. An outbreak of cholera had claimed the lives of 14 villagers between July and October 1832.

A 90-year-old lady, Mrs. Ellis née Weedon, when returning to her place of birth in Hall End, which at that time was a little hamlet of 14 thatched cottages including the now demolished *Harrow Inn*, recalled that only one well had to meet the whole demand for them and the Lower Road cottages including the Bunch. When it ran dry in the summer, which was often, water had to be carried long distances in pails and buckets. The brook at Hall End and the same brook higher up at Marsh Lane and the Risborough Road was used as in particularly dry summers most of the wells in the village failed. Thus it was no surprise that in 1898 the Aylesbury Rural District Council told the parish council of the medical officer for health's report which had stated that the drinking water of the village was of an insufficient and impure nature.

The chairman of the council, J. H. Tapping, told the meeting at which the letter was read that a supply of good water could be obtained by deepening the shallow wells in the parish. At the same time the clerk was asked to ascertain what the Chiltern Hills Spring Water Company would charge for their water to be laid into the village. In their reply the company said that this could be done for £1,000. Sir Oswald Mosley, a local landowner living at Whitethorn House, had offered £250 towards the cost and the company itself would help out with another £250, leaving the balance to be found by the parish.

This estimate was carefully examined and it was asked whether the pipes would be laid throughout the length of the parish for this price. Mr. Tapping also returned to the matter of deepening the existing wells. Had they been looked after properly, he said, there would have been no difficulty. Mr. James Spittles, another councillor, agreed that there was a good number of wells which always gave a plentiful supply. Other councillors, however, were of the opinion that the benefit to the community would outweigh the few years' increased cost to the ratepayers, estimated at 6d. in the pound. So a circular letter was sent to the property owners explaining the position and asking for contributions towards the parish's share.

The subsequent response was poor so it was proposed that the shortfall should be raised by a loan, and the clerk was instructed to ask the Chiltern Hills Spring Water Company to proceed with the project. By October 1900, however, the cost of installation had gone up to £1,150 and the council decided to pull out unless the company could adhere to their original estimate.

Stoke Mandeville Parish Council.

AYLESBURY

November 24th, 1899.

DEAR SIR,

The Report of the Medical Officer of Health, made to the Aylesbury Rural District Council, that "the drinking water of Stoke Mandeville is of an insufficient and impure nature," has rendered it imperative that steps shall be taken to procure a sufficient supply of good drinking water for the Parish.

At a conference between this Council and a Committee of the Rural District Council, held here on Wednesday, the 22nd inst., the question of how best to get this supply was fully considered.

It was, in the end, generally agreed that if the water of the Chiltern Hills Spring Water Company could be laid into the Parish, without largely increasing the Rates which are already heavy, it would be the best way of obtaining the required supply of good drinking water.

The Engineer of the Company estimates the cost of laying on this water, throughout the Parish, at £1,000.

Towards this amount the Company itself would contribute £250, and Sir Oswald Mosley, who owns two farms in the Parish, has also very liberally offered £250.

Now as the laying on of a reliable supply of good water into the Parish would greatly increase the value of house property, and of land, especially **of land well situated for Building purposes**, the Parish Council confidently appeals to the Owners to contribute liberally towards the amount of £500 required to make up the cost of getting this water here.

Unless a liberal response is made to this appeal, the Parish Council will feel itself bound—in the interests of the Ratepayers—to oppose the proposal to lay on the Chiltern Hills water, as being too expensive.

Kindly give this matter your careful consideration, and advise the Council at your earliest convenience of the amount you yourself will be prepared to contribute.

We are, DEAR SIR,

Your obedient Servants,

J. H. TAPPING, *Chairman.*
C. E. ARNOLD, *Clerk.*

26. The circular letter to ratepayers seeking contributions towards a piped water supply, 1899.

It was another year before things started to move again. The company had come back with a counter suggestion. They were willing to supply metered water, for no less than seven years, to the parish boundary, subject to an annual fee of £100 for up to a third of a million gallons and 1s. 6d. per thousand gallons thereafter. After due consideration, the council decided that this scheme was impracticable and that they expected the water company to lay and manage the supply at their previous estimate. They added a rider that if a reasonable agreement could not be reached, the parish was confident that they could obtain a supply of water within the parish itself. This, in retrospect, was probably a bit of bluff as the councillors did not have enough knowledge to proceed with a scheme of their own.

In November 1902, four years after the medical officer's report on the state of the water supply at Stoke Mandeville was made, the rural district council decided that enough was enough and that a local government board should enquire into all aspects of the affair. The particular point of dispute was the need for a loan over and above the contributions from property owners, which had been very poor, and the parish council decided to oppose such a loan because of its burden upon the rates.

The enquiry opened in the village at the end of November. The local press was there and the *Bucks Herald* gave a very vivid account of the proceedings. It seems that the villagers were out in force and were divided into two opposing camps as the reporter made it clear, for it was 'of a far more lively character than such functions usually present'. The verbal battle raged, and 'for every witness who was ready to declare that the supply [of water] was urgently needed, there was another who was equally positive that there was either no necessity for it at all or that the particular method of supplying it was the most undesirable of all'. Such were the demonstrations, for and against, that the Inspector was compelled to remind the public mildly that 'the inquiry was not exactly a concert and that applause was therefore out of place'.

The outcome seems to have been that they would sanction the scheme, provided alterations could be made so that the present main would be extended just inside the parish boundary on the Lower Road. If you could not, or the landlord would not, extend the supply to your own residence, the standpipe, positioned at eight places, had to be used: the borough boundary near Bedgrove and the Hospital, respectively; the Hall End turning; the Lower Road below the *Bell*; at Chapel Lane; the corner near the church; the Wendover Road near the former post office; and Station Road near Plested's.

But old habits die hard and it was not long before complaints were made about the quality of the water and the sites of the hydrants. The water was said to be discoloured with a muddy sediment and it was suggested that the pipes needed to be flushed out. This was a very wasteful method of supply for children often left the taps running and there were many bursts in frosty weather.

Until the beginning of the Second World War, the rural district council paid a contractor to cover over the stanchions with straw and sacking but even this was not a complete success.

The position of the hydrant near the *Bell* also came in for criticism and it was thought that unless it was moved it would be a serious impediment to traffic, 'several vehicles having been already delayed in passing the spot'. An alternative position, between the school and the allotment gate, was suggested but the rural district council refused to agree to this. There were also complaints that persons outside the village had been illegally using and carrying away water from the hydrants, and steps were taken to prevent 'this illegal use and the waste of water by careless or mischievous users'. The key of the supply was handed to a councillor with instructions on how to use it.

In 1903 Sir Oswald Mosley's agent asked the water company for pipes to be laid to his cottages, but the company secretary was instructed to advise him that the company had nothing to do with the pipes beyond the parish boundary. Interestingly it was recorded by the late Reg Bunce of the Lee, who was born at the Bell Inn where his father, William, was the landlord, that his father was employed to dig by hand a trench for the pipes from the nearest point to the parish boundary and then on the grass verges in the principal roads. For this work he was paid 6d. per chain (22 yards). Once the trench work had been carried out, the actual plumbing and laying of the pipes, after the water company declined to oblige, was done by Messrs. Webster and Cannon of Aylesbury.

So it was that the piped water supply came into the village at the eight standpipes, some of which were still in use 40 years later, the last being the one outside the parish church.

Sewerage and Refuse

The introduction of a sewage system in Stoke had a less stormy passage although it took 10 years. The Second World War undoubtedly interrupted its progress. Before this the rural district council had engaged a Mr. Saunders of Wendover to empty any household cesspits. This was done by inserting a long hose and sucking the effluent into a special horse-drawn tank. As the hose was often full of holes, much of the contents spilled on to the road. Those without cesspits had to dispose of the 'privy' waste as best they could.

In March 1936 a deputation met the council and their request for a parish meeting to discuss a scheme of sewerage was agreed. Such a scheme was drawn up but deferred because of the war. Directly after the end of hostilities, when the number of houses in the village was increasing, it was realised that the question of main drainage was becoming urgent and in May 1946 the council were demanding more information on the subject from the authorities. The deferred plan was brought out and dusted down, and tenders were put out for the work. In February 1947, however, the Rev. Frederick Winterton, who represented the village on the rural district council, reported that the preliminaries were in hand, but it took another three years or so before the sewers were working.

There was no door to door collection of refuse available to the villagers before the Second World War. The council was asked by the rural district council in the 1930s to consider the question of a dump in the village 'as, owing to the rapid development of property, the present conditions were most unsatisfactory and detrimental to health'. As there was no land available, the council suggested that perhaps adjacent Weston Turville's dump could be used for a reasonable price. Periodic collection of 'Hardware Refuse' was mooted with a rental of £3 per annum for the site and a tender for collection of 15s. per day. The ever helpful Councillor William Tapping offered to loan a piece of land *gratis* in Hall End Lane provided a hole was dug and the refuse buried, but this offer was never taken up.

Municipal Housing

The tied cottage of the agricultural labourer had long been a feature of village life but was gradually being phased out at the beginning of the 1900s. The need for reasonably priced rented accommodation still remained, however, and the rural district councils became involved as the First World War drew to a close. The parish council was asked to estimate the number of additional houses that would be needed for the 'working classes' after the war. This they put at 'a few', restricted to the occupation of agricultural workers. They were then asked to select various sites in the parish for the erection of 20 additional houses and four sites were chosen on the Lower Road and one adjoining the Wesleyan Chapel.

A further development was afoot in 1925 when, in response to a circular letter, it was said that four houses were requisite. In 1931 the rural district council was ready to purchase land and Mr. William Tapping sold a plot in Lower Road at a cost of £400. A block contract had been given to a London firm to build council houses at £199 each in various villages throughout the Aylesbury rural district including Weston Turville and Stoke Mandeville and 10 were erected on the land sold by Mr. Tapping. When the village was connected to the sewers, bathrooms were added to the houses. A full modernisation of these properties was undertaken in 1986-7 including re-roofing. The cost of this per unit was £16,183, such has been inflation in the intervening years.

Along Station Road 20 properties had been built in the mid- 1920s and their address was just 'The Council Houses'. As the village grew, however, it was thought that the junction should have a name and, in 1946, Hampden Road was decided upon. The first phase of the new housing estate in Eskdale Road was nearing completion in 1949-50 when the first 10 were ready, and further followed in the next decade. Such was the delay, however, that in 1947 six houses in Castle Park, Wendover were offered to Stoke residents.

27. The council houses, c.1930.

The shortage after the war of both materials and labour was plain for all to see and the housing crisis was still very acute. In 1951 a suggestion that the vicarage, which had been empty for many months after Mr. Winterton's retirement and before the new incumbent's appointment, should be turned into flats and a small house or bungalow found for the new man, was politely rejected by the Dean of Lincoln.

The bungalows at the second roundabout in Eskdale Road were ready in 1952 but progress was slow elsewhere in the road and in 1955 one councillor commented that he was amazed that it took over 12 months to build six houses. The council's attention was drawn to the older houses in Hampden Road where there was no electricity in the bedrooms, the tenant being reliant on candles, a most dangerous situation especially for children. As new property became available, the Hampden Road houses were demolished and the occupants rehoused. In 1975, in spite of opposition, 10 garages in Eskdale Road were demolished to make room for old people's bungalows.

Allocation of the new properties, as and when they came available, was also a subject of friction with charges of unfairness, a subject to which the council returned again and again over the years.

Street Lighting
At the beginning of 1927, the Aylesbury Borough Council electrical engineers asked the parish council to consider the question of public street lighting. An

estimate of the costs revealed that if the lamp was lit from half an hour after sun-set until 1.30 a.m. and from 5 a.m. until half an hour before sunrise, the electricity used at 1d. per unit and a standing charge for the lamp and bulb would amount to £3 5s. per lamp per annum. It was suggested that there should be six lamps in the village.

The parish council thought the sum excessive and suggested a figure of £3 per lamp. This was agreed upon by the electricity company but lights were to go out at 11.30 p.m. rather than 1.30 a.m. Matters were deferred, however, on the grounds of economy, as it would have cost a 2d. rate and it was not until 1934 that, by adopting the Lighting and Watching Act of 1833, the village streets were finally 'lit up'. The parish council is still responsible for lighting within the village.

Postal Services

It was in 1900 that the parish council decided to make formal application for the establishment of a post office at Stoke Mandeville and within a month sanction had been given by the G.P.O. in London. The office was established at Fleet Cottage and William Mason was the first postmaster. Until then there had been a wall box and the postal collection and delivery was made by 'foot messenger' from Aylesbury. At that time Fleet Cottage stood right back from the road and was approached by a long path. It was not long before there were complaints about the path to the box, which was by the church, and a request was made to the county surveyor for the roadway to be made good.

The Aylesbury postmaster was anxious to ease the postman's working day and in 1924 asked if the parish council would have any objection to an earlier collection of letters on Saturday evenings. The suggestion for the box to be emptied at 1.45 p.m. instead of the usual 6 p.m. was opposed and it was another three years before the council agreed to the postman having a half day on Thurdays. Some years earlier the local office had been given permission to have half day closing.

Burial Ground

In 1934 a parish meeting was called at which the vicar stated that the church-yard was almost full up, and in order for it to be extended a sum of £300 would be required. It was up to the electorate to agree what steps should be taken. By an overwhelming vote, it was decided to adopt the Burial Act so that a burial ground could be instigated.

There were only five grave spaces left in 1936, and as this was the estimated number of interments per year, it was agreed to authorise the parish council to borrow £150 to purchase a piece of land for burial purposes, provided the site met with the approval of the Minister of Health.

The land decided upon was in Swallow Lane and owned by Malthouse Farm; the total cost including the fencing was £240. Burial fees were also considered and these were 13s. for digging a 5ft. grave, 4s. for the minister and 5s. to the parish council. Double fees were charged for non-parishioners. Exclusive rights of burials were also agreed upon at £2 2s. and 5s. each in respect of headstone and curb.

Parish Welfare and Health in the Village

The parish has been responsible for the well-being of its inhabitants from Elizabethan times right up to the last century when poor law administration was taken over by the commissioners who organised parishes into unions for the purpose of poor relief. Stoke Mandeville fell within the Saunderton Union until 1896 when it was transferred to that of Aylesbury.

The administration at a local level was undertaken by the overseers of the poor, a poor rate being levied on property. In 1824, for example, a rate of 1s. in the pound was being sought and the charges ranged from £17 10s. 9d. from the chief landowner at the time, Thomas Ligo Webb to 3d. from William Langston, a village labourer who possessed a cottage. Ninety years later a figure of 2s. in the pound was being charged on buildings not classified for agriculture, and half that figure on agricultural ones.

The overseers' account book contains some interesting entries and gives a revealing picture of life in the early part of the last century. The poor had nowhere to turn but the parish and posterity must judge whether it failed the community as a forerunner to the welfare state. There can be no doubt that at the local level the parish tried to look after its own, within what it saw as its limited responsibilities and resources. The same cannot be said of the workhouse unions after 1834.

From the account book for the year 1827, when over £30 per month was being spent in needy cases, the following is gleaned at random:

> Mending Martha Harding's shoes – 1s.: Joseph Dodd, new pair of shoes – 14s. 4d.: 2s. Mutton for broth: Paid the women for laying Thos. Mason out – 5s.

An orphaned family was a drain on parish finances until the children were working or could be apprenticed, but in the meantime the children had to be looked after. The fortunes of the Forster family can be traced in this manner:

> Paid the women for laying out Forster's wife - 1s.
> James Fleet's wife. Making shroud for Forster - 1s.
> Bear [Beer] Bread and Cheese for Forster's funeral - 5s. 2d.
> Washing Forster's boys - 1s.
> Paid Mrs. Smith for doing for the Forsters - 1s.

Before the advent of the national health service, villages relied heavily on their district nurse to advise on routine health matters. Nurses were organised in the county by the Buckinghamshire District Nursing Association, which was established in 1909 and affiliated to the Queen's Institute the following year (becoming the Queen Victoria's Jubilee Institute for Nurses). Subscribers paid as little as 5s. per annum, and, as the nurse was on call at all times of the day and night, she had to be resident in the village. In Stoke Mandeville, the Association owned a bungalow at 53 Risborough Road in which the village's nurse lived. Sisters Evans and Holder are but two names remembered from this devoted body of professionals.

The local health authority purchased the property when the national health service was established in 1948 and the proceeds were invested in a charity fund – The Weston Turville and Stoke Mandeville District Nursing Association – which was later renamed the Weston Turville and Stoke Mandeville Aid in Sickness Fund, which is still one of the parish charities.

Chapter Ten

Roads and Transport

There is no detailed map surviving in this country for Stoke Mandeville before 1798 and earlier ones hardly mention the village. The enclosure map of this date, from which so much information in this work has been taken, shows, two roads, as now, running north and south. The one to the west is the Wycombe to Aylesbury road and the one to the east joins Wendover to Aylesbury with a track, later to become the New Road and then renamed Station Road, completing the letter H. Along these two roads came the main traffic, such as it was. They were also linked by a bridle path, which went in a north-easterly direction through Johnson's Castle Field to the Wendover Road opposite, or somewhat north of, the County Farm site, then called Stoke Close and owned by the Mercers' Company. The track was diverted to the east when the railway was built at the end of the last century, and now forms part of the existing bridleway.

Another track is said to have linked the two roads, starting in the centre of the village behind the *Bull* and coming out near the Marrow Way in Wendover Road. Parts of it are shown on the first edition of the old series of Ordnance Survey maps where the track from Stoke House goes out to the Wendover Road. All these paths were disturbed when the railway was built and numbers of the old twisty lanes, which had already been blocked off by order of the Enclosure Commissioners, soon disappeared altogether when they were not used.

In the mid-1800s The Sovereign, the London to Leamington coach, ran through the parish along the Wendover Road 'every afternoon' but there would have been few passengers on it for Stoke. A gig also went every afternoon from the *King's Head* in Aylesbury to High Wycombe, via Wendover and Great Missenden, but anyone travelling to Stoke Mandeville would have been dropped at the Stoke Turn.

There were also a number of carriers who transported the occasional passenger as well as goods to and from the outlying places but there was no regular service as such apart from the Baker family, who plied from Stoke to London on Tuesdays and Thursdays about this time on a route which has not been recorded. They also undertook a Saturday afternoon trip from the *Bull's Head Inn* out of Aylesbury to Stoke at 3 p.m., and this must have taken villagers home after market day. They would have come along the Lower Road. Another service later in the century came from Princes Risborough into Aylesbury on

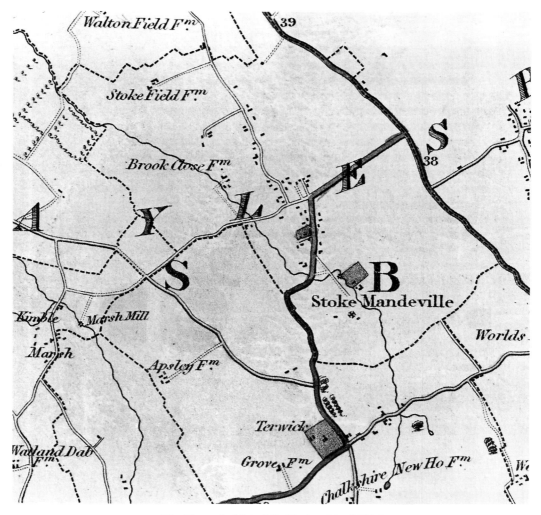

28. Bryant's *Map of Buckinghamshire*, 1824-5.

Wednesdays and Saturdays, and the obvious route through the village via Terrick toll gate is confirmed by directories of this date.

The two 'main' roads, which were the responsibility of the turnpike authorities, came under the auspices of the county council in 1891, although the other roads continued within the domain of the parish until 1895 when they were taken over by the newly formed urban and rural district councils.

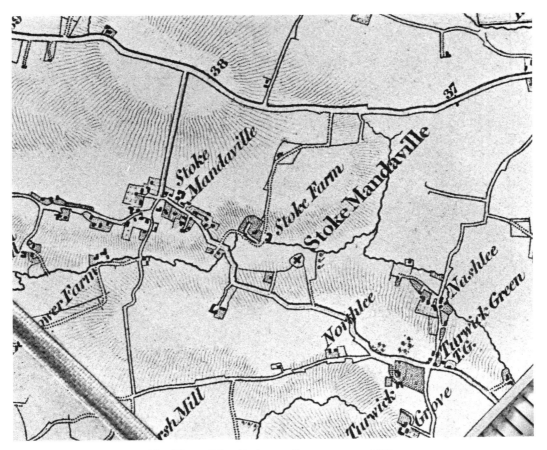

29. First edition Ordnance Survey map, *c.*1830.

It is clear that as far back as 1720 the authorities were taking an interest in the state of the Wendover Road. In that year an Act for the repairing of the road had been passed: '... by reason of the many heavy carriages frequently passing through same, it has become so ruinous and bad that in the winter season the said road is very dangerous to travellers'. The trustees appointed to rectify the situation included Thomas Ligo gent. of Stoke Mandeville, and it is thought that the Causeway, as the Wendover Road was called very early on, was built up at this time in an attempt to escape the clay base of the road. In very much earlier times the route taken by all travellers was the Icknield Way and the nearest point of this ancient track to the village was at Terrick on its way from the Kimbles.

The route then went along the present World's End Lane and on into Weston Turville.

The inhabitants of the parishes through which the roads passed were required to help out with the maintenance. In 1801 each received a notice informing them of their legal responsibilities in that they were '... liable or subject in law to do statute work for the present year upon the road ... or to the payments of any money in lieu of'. In 1830 another Act was passed 'for the more effectively repairing the Wendover to Buckingham Turnpike Road'. This turnpike trust was wound up in 1878.

As far as the Risborough to Aylesbury via 'Kimbel' route is concerned, the account book of the 'Payments to Labourers' for 1796 is preserved, but again it is not clear whether the route from Terrick Gate went via World's End Lane and Weston Turville on the old Icknield Way or through Stoke. Some of the entries are quite interesting. One page headed 'Carting Don on the Risbrow Road' showed that the labourer's daily rate was 1s. Other entries included the surveyor's dinner, 1s., and other amounts for 'Super and Licker'. It was obviously thirsty work on the Buckinghamshire roads.

In 1825 another Act of Parliament was enacted 'for more effectively repairing and improving certain roads passing through Princes Risborough in the County of Buckinghamshire and communicating with Aylesbury and Great Marlow and Thame'. The toll house on this route is now the cottage next to the garage at Terrick. The route is then thought to have continued through Stoke Mandeville and the Lower Road into Aylesbury at Walton where there was another toll house, now a cottage in the middle of the gyratory system.

Within the confines of Stoke Mandeville, however, the Commissioners of the earlier Enclosure Act defined the roads in the village as:

1. The Public Carriage Road from Aylesbury to Wendover.

2. From the North corner of the Common Fields of Ellesborough in an North East direction along Blessbury Lane to Stoke Green and across the said Green over Castle Field to Turnpike Road, one and a half furlongs Aylesbury side of the 38th milestone.

3. From North East of Blessbury Lane in North West direction along side of Stoke Green into Common Fields of Walton.

4. From North corner of Stoke Green to the South corner into a lane towards Ellesborough.

5. Bridle Road from Common Fields of Walton at North Corner of Mead Furlong and Home Meadow towards Marsh.

From this valuable summary, which was far more informative than any map of the day could be, the roads can be identified as:

1. The Wendover Road.

2. Marsh Lane into the village and then Bridle Path no. 1 which started along the hedge in Station Road (at 35, currently Mr. Lane's property) out to the

Wendover Road at County Farm.
3. Lower Road.
4. Risborough Road.
5. The edge of what is now Hawkeslade Estate and the paths out towards Standall's Farm and Marsh. (Stoke 16 and Stone 19.)

It is interesting to note that whenever or wherever a dispute arose concerning the state of the roads, or ditches alongside them, it was always up to the other party to rectify matters. At the very first working meeting of the newly established parish council in 1895, the 'dangerous condition of the ditch at the turning on the highway opposite Stoke Church' was brought to the attention of the county surveyor. A month later the response came that 'the ditch near the church complained of at the last meeting was for the most part on a parish highway for which the parish surveyors were alone responsible ...'. Later the same year open ditches and drains were again discussed, in particular the bad state of the ditch from Joe's Close to Butt's Pond and its continuation from the Bull Inn Yard to Butt's Pond. The county surveyor was again advised of the situation with a view to remedying the nuisance and, on this occasion, the reply must have been positive for no further steps were recommended.

The transport of the country was at this time (the turn of the century) changing from horses and carts into the mechanised age of motor cars and this was, in its way, not only a revolution for the village but also a revelation to its inhabitants. Neither the roads nor the disposition of the villagers seemed able to cope with the rapidly changing situation.

In 1910 Councillor Christopher Arnold, who was the headmaster (1894-1914) of the local board school, said that a playing field was necessary, 'owing to the high speed of motors through the village making it unsafe for the children to play in the roads'. A similar request in the form of a petition the year before had been turned down as there was no land available. The council also recommended 'motor danger signals' at the turnings near the church and school and the county agreed to this request. Lower Road too had become a problem and the council asked for it to be taken over by the county as it was 'being used practically as a main road'.

Some years later, in 1921, Councillor Samuel Johnson, Mr. Arnold's son-in-law, who lived at Bushey Cottage on the corner of Swallow Lane and Station Road, reported that 'at the turning of the main road near the church, several motorists have lost their bearings and entered Swallow Lane to the danger of the public'. The clerk was instructed to ask the county 'to cause to be erected a sign distinguishing the route at this junction in order to prevent a recurrence of these mistakes'.

The following year there were more complaints about the same junction and 'the dangerous pace that motorists rounded the corner near Mr. Pargeter's shop'. The help of the Automobile Association scout was sought with a view to

30. Station Road looking east, *c.*1930.

31. Station Road looking west, *c.*1930.

erecting a sign. Nothing seems to have been done, however, for in 1924 Councillor Johnson raised the matter again, owing to the vast amount of motor traffic that passes this spot daily'.

Omnibuses were beginning to link the villages and, with the troublesome corner still in mind, a letter was sent to the Highways Committee in 1926 protesting against the proposed service between Wycombe and Aylesbury via Stoke using that section of the road, until the 'corner and surface of the road be placed in a satisfactory condition'. The matter was still unresolved four years later but lack of funds was still the reason for no action.

Much has been said elsewhere and far more eloquently about the Metropolitan Railway but this chapter on roads and transport could not be complete without mention of the railway at Stoke. The line from Baker Street was not extended from Chesham to Aylesbury until 1892 and there was much excitement on the day that the new 16-mile stretch was opened. On Thursday 1 September a special train left Baker Street station for Aylesbury, albeit somewhat late, with a party of directors and railway officials including the dynamic chairman, Sir Edward Watkin, who was the driving force behind the project. At every station on the line the train was received with enthusiasm, particularly at Wendover. The *Daily Telegraph* reporter commented: ' If it had not been for the opposition of the landowners years ago George Stephenson's railway would have embraced Wendover in his London and North Western route, and today, instead of a picturesquely-situated hamlet surrounded by high hills, we might have seen a flourishing centre of population'. Quite how the London paper's comments were received in representing the former parliamentary borough as a hamlet is not noted but the reporter was no more generous in describing the next station along the line as 'within the parish in which most of the so called Aylesbury ducks are reared' – nor more accurate. The local paper was a little more accommodating but the reporter could not resist a snide comment or two:

> We are informed that 71 booked for the first journey which left Aylesbury at 7.13 a.m., the great majority of whom got out at Stoke or Wendover, though a few continued to Baker Street. A punctual start was made and shortly after the village of Stoke Mandeville received its first railway train. For a village, Stoke may said to have one of the largest, most comfortable stations to be found anywhere. In the event of the dwelling houses being destroyed by fire or flood, the whole of the inhabitants can find temporary shelter in the station buildings. But we stay less time at Stoke Mandeville than it takes to write about it.

To begin with there were eight stopping trains every day including Sundays, but certainly in later years, after Marylebone Station had been built in 1899 and the connection made with the Midlands via Verney Junction, fast through trains did not stop at Stoke.

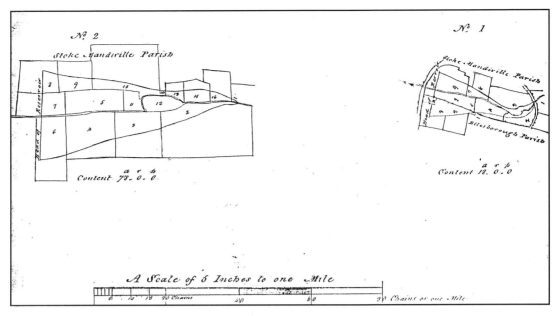

32. Plan of proposed feeder reservoirs, 1813.

33. Siting of proposed reservoirs, 1813.

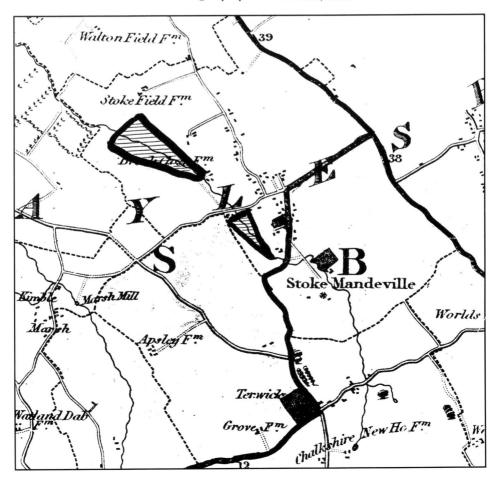

In 1913 the parish council wrote to the Metropolitan and Great Central Railway Company asking for a later train to be put on at night so that people attending theatres and other places of amusement could get a train home from Aylesbury. This request was refused. Another approach was made in 1915 after an alteration to the timetable had been made. The council asked for the 10.15 a.m. train from Marylebone, which passed through the station about 11.25 a.m., to be stopped at Stoke. This request was also refused on the grounds that 'a number of gentlemen attending the County Council meetings being held at 11.30 a.m. travel by this train'.

Through trains to the Midlands via Aylesbury ceased running in 1966, but many still remember the pleasure of a leisurely afternoon tea in the dining car on the South Yorkshireman which ran daily between London Marylebone and Bradford Exchange. Aylesbury was reached in under an hour and in 1959 the set afternoon tea on this restaurant car express cost 3s.

A mode of transport which nearly affected Stoke Mandeville was the canal system. As an early forerunner of the railways, canals became very important in the 18th century and carried heavy traffic economically. The opening of the Aylesbury arm of the Grand Junction is said to have halved the cost of coal in the town.

In 1813 detailed plans were drawn up for a new canal to join the Wilts. and Berks. Canal at Abingdon with the Grand Junction at Marsworth. It would have followed the course of the Bear Brook past Haydon Mill through Stone, Dinton and Cuddington parishes to Thame, Wheatley and on to Culham on the River Thames.

The intention was to build two feeder reservoirs and this was where Stoke Mandeville would have come in, for both were to have been sited within the parish. Their total area was some 96 acres and would have incorporated the Stoke Brook which runs in a north-westerly direction until it joins the Bear Brook at Haydon Mill close to the River Thame.

In the plan the tail of the larger of the reservoirs started at Old Moat Farm, and passed through the fields for two thirds of a mile, ending about five hundred feet short of what later became Stoke Farm. It was 1,500 ft. long at its head. Had the plan come to fruition, the railway to Princes Risborough and High Wycombe could never have taken its present route. The smaller reservoir was planned to have its tail on the old Risborough Road and, like its sister, to run north-westerly towards Marsh Lane, finishing just short of Brook Farm. It would have been 1,800 ft. in length and 800 ft. at the head.

The plan, however, never left the drawing board as the Grand Junction Canal Company was less than enthusiastic about it. Their particular worry was that the volume of water required for the scheme was more than the proposed reservoirs could supply.

Perhaps the village should be grateful that the scheme never saw the light of day, for with two reservoirs in place, Stoke Mandeville would have developed in a very different manner from today.

Chapter Eleven

Sports and Social Recreation

Cricket and Football

Football and cricket have been played locally for many years and one meadow in particular, called the Butts, was used quite regularly by the cricket team. This can be identified as part of four acres of land belonging to Butts Farm (probably called Corner Farm in census records) which stretched from Station Road to Risborough Road behind the *Bull,* and formed part of what is now Brudenell Drive. The farmhouse had gone by 1910 and the land was described as meadow and sheds in the taxation returns. The Butts' Farm House, which was thought to be an earlier name for the original Oak Tree Farm House, stood a little way from the present house of that name, which was built about 1851 and enlarged just before the Second World War.

In earlier days cricket was always more popular than football in the villages, a flat field, ball and wickets being all that was needed, whereas organised football, where the crowd participation was such an important part of the proceedings, was less so until more recent times. The cricket team always contained a good cross-section of the community and in those class-ridden Victorian days it must have been very satisfactory for the keen farm labourer or blacksmith to dismiss the local squire or important farmer for a 'duck'. In looking through some of the newspaper reports of village matches, it seems that the Stoke lads were keen but kamikaze in their behaviour and that Bishopstone in particular always seemed to be a match for them.

On one particular occasion in 1874, the home team put the visitors in and Bishopstone made 159, of which Crook, their opening batsman, made 116, although four of his team were out without score. When it came to Stoke's turn they made 51 in the first innings and 27 in the follow on, only one player in each innings making double figures – 10 on each occasion.

Moving on to this century, in the 1920s both football and cricket prospered in the village, with mostly the same players in both sports. A story is told of a lovely sunny day in the '30s when the team was playing at home to Buckland on the Pond Mead pitch. Their rivals had a strong side, composed mostly of players from Aston Clinton, and they had thrashed Stoke on their home ground earlier in the season. On the return match the home team had struggled to a total of 104 runs all out. Tea was being taken at the *Woolpack Inn* nearby when a sudden

34. The Cricket Club, 1952. Back row, from left: J. Webb, H. Allen, W. Budd, J. Fountaine, A. Miles, W. Bamford, G. Halsey, F. Carter; front row: S. Allen, T. Blair, J. Miles, R. Prior, T. Cumer.

35. Winners of the Aylesbury and District Football League 1928-9. Back row, from left: Mr. Purssell, D. Rushworth, A. Bateman, H. Hern, ? Rushworth, C. Janes, W. Bateman; centre row: ? Bunce, T. Taylor, F. Ellis, J. Edmonds, A. Bateman; front row: ? Faulkner, B. Tuckey.

downpour struck the village, immediately followed by blazing sunshine, which made the pitch quite unplayable. Buckland were dismissed in a few overs for four, all extras, not one Buckland player managing to score. The following week's *Bucks Herald* ran the headline, 'BUCKLAND IS NOW DUCKLAND'.

The Stoke Mandeville team won the Aylesbury and District Football League in 1928-9 although it must be said that some of the players were from outside the village.

Fair Time

The piece of land referred to above as the Butts had been used for many years for all sorts of other social activities. Every August Bank Holiday Monday there would be a fair with all the associated fun and games; bowling for a pig, climbing the greasy pole and a sheaf tossing competition, as well as all the usual races for young and old alike, and tradition has it that in the 1920s the event attracted many thousands of visitors who arrived in packed trains.

In the sheaf tossing, an obviously rustic sport, two poles were dug into the ground a dozen or so feet apart and between them a bar was suspended at a considerable height. The competitors were given one or two unthreshed wheat sheaves tied in a sack which they had to throw with a pitchfork cleanly over the suspended bar. If more than one managed to toss the sheaf successfully, the first prize went to the one whose sheaf landed the greatest distance on the other side.

This was not a competition of great strength but a pitchfork with both prongs worn wafer thin and an ability to flick the sheaf a long distance with a turn of the wrist, were essential. This sport was very popular in all country districts in the south of England before the First World War.

Another rural competition, more linked to everyday work than play, and recorded at Stoke Mandeville, was that of horseshoe-making by farriers or their assistants. They were required to fix a shoe and then pass an oral examination on the anatomy and structure of the leg or foot of a horse. The winners were allowed to keep the horse shoes they had made as souvenirs and the county prizewinner received a leather apron. The youngest was given a farrier's knife.

Horticultural and Cottagers' Shows

The Church, in earlier days, involved itself in organising social events. By taking a lead, where frequently no other was forthcoming, the clergy, and more often their wives, ensured that everything was conducted in a sober and orderly manner without a hint of impropriety, and a high moral tone was usually struck. That is not to say that young people did not enjoy themselves as young people do nor that home-made wine and cider did not flow when the occasion warranted it.

The Cottagers' Show became a regular annual event in Mr. Partington's time. Its stated objects were 'to promote habits of industry amongst the working class by offering prizes for the best horticultural productions'. Another feature was a prize for the best piece of needlework and the best made shirt suitable for a working man, so as to 'fit the labourers' daughters for labourers' wives'.

The Rev. Mr. Partington gave a suitable homily in 1860. 'All felt grateful to the Ruler of All Seasons in his mercy for giving them all a fine day. A great deal arose from such Societies as those for it was by the Clergy uniting with the Laity and by the rich meeting the poor, that the country would be improved.' He also expressed the opinion that if master and men were thrown together more often it would be the means of ending the strikes which had occurred of late in the metropolis.

A hundred years later, the villagers were still showing off their skills, although in a more relaxed manner. No longer under the eye of the Church authorities, the shows had become very much more secular affairs. But support was still patchy and varying degrees of success were reported. At the A.G.M. of the Gardens and Allotments Association in 1966 it was reported that the entries were declining and that the Association had not done so well during the year. There was apathy in the village over the show, said the retiring secretary, and more people had to become interested. The annual subscription was increased from 1s. to 2s.6d. A year later an improvement was reported with a membership of fifty. It was said in 1968 that the exhibits for the show were as good as ever but the storm, that had kept people away, had washed out the sideshows and a loss of £11 had been incurred. Where have the horticultural shows gone in the 1990s?

Harvest Home

Harvest Home was a traditional way of celebrating a job well done, for, in the early days, nearly everyone was involved in one way or another with the gathering in of the harvest in villages such as Stoke Mandeville. The harvest home feast, at least, still continues to be held.

A typical celebration took place and was recorded on an October Tuesday in 1875. The day started with an 11 a.m. service, and the report in the local paper was forced to admit that 'the congregation might have been larger. Next year we hope to see it so'. One hundred and twenty sat down in a spacious tent provided by the caterers, Messrs. Garners of Aylesbury, to partake of 'as nice a collation as anyone could wish to see and everything was done justice to'. Tea was served to 200 after the youngsters had had their play time and then it was ready for the bells to ring the summons for Evensong. 'The choir led the processional hymn, ''Onward Christian Soldiers' and here we cannot help saying how really creditably the choir managed their part in the service. It only shows what country men and lads can do if they give their minds to a thing.'

36.   The village bellringers *c*.1913. Back row, from left: S. Johnson, ?, D. Spence, H. J. Strong; centre row: B. Spittles, C. Spence, G. Smith, E. Bateman, ?, ?, J. Tomkins, F. Purssell; front row: C. E. Arnold, J. Stilton, W. Winterton, the Rev. F. J. Winterton, P. Purssell, J. H. Tapping, H. Rutland.

A new feature of the church was a reredos entirely painted by the vicar and Mrs. Hanson. 'In the centre over the altar is the Lamb in white, the ground throughout being a blue grey dispersed alternatively with the leaf and flower of the passion plant. It must be pronounced a great success and encouragement to all amateurs in such work'. The new vicar and his wife had not taken long to

show their artistic talents but there were still those who resented outsiders inter-
fering and trying to change things.

Penny Readings and Village Treats

Penny Readings were popular over many decades and also seem to have been
introduced by Edward Hanson. The *Bucks Herald* again: 'The Penny Readings
held in the school on the Tuesday before Christmas Day proved quite a success,
and the room being crowded with a large and highly satisfied audience'.

A subscription list was often started to finance such entertainment which otherwise would have been impossible to arrange. One such list in 1867 was headed
by two guineas from Lady de Rothschild of Tring Park, whose husband had just
begun to buy land in the parish, and the Christmas treat consisted of a tree
laden with gifts for the children who were allowed two presents each as well as
an excellent tea with a 'double allowance of cake and wine'.

In Dr. Mensor's day, the Sunday school appears to have been particularly well
attended, probably because his treats were generous affairs. Shortly after his
appointment as vicar, the *Bucks Herald* was able to report the first of many:

> The schoolroom was handsomely decorated for the occasion with banners, ever-
> greens and flowers. The teachers and children assembled at 2 p.m. in the school
> and after their names had been called they marched in procession, headed by an
> elegant banner, to the vicarage lawn singing, 'Brightly gleams our banner'. When
> they had finished singing the hymn, the banner was placed on the lawn and the
> children began to play. At 4 o'clock they returned to the school and after grace
> had been sung, sat down at four long tables to a beautiful repast consisting of roast
> beef, plum pudding, tea, cakes etc. provided by Mrs. Mensor being her gift to the
> Sunday scholars. Tea being over, the children retired to play on the lawn and the
> teachers and friends were then fed. In the evening there was an entertainment to
> which the parents were invited. The Rev. Dr. Mensor gave an appropriate address
> which was attentively listened to and the children sang hymns and school songs in
> a manner which gave great satisfaction.

Working Men's Association and the Social Sons of Harmony

An effort was made at this time to start up a Working Men's Association. In
October of 1882, their winter session commenced with a tea in the National
schoolroom at which Mrs. Mensor presided. After this Dr. Mensor proposed the
health of the Queen and Royal Family. He exhorted his hearers not to be led
away by agitators but to hold fast to the time-honoured constitution. The President then proposed 'Success to the Working Men's Association' and begged the
working men to avail themselves of the advantages offered them. He would not
go as far as to teach total abstinence but it behoved all to be temperate, and if
the warm room and company of the public house constituted the chief attraction, they might find superior comfort and more rational amusement at the
meeting of the association.

Another organisation in the village seems to have been the Social Sons of Harmony who, reading between the lines, had the same overall objects as the Working Men's Association and were a bit put out that rivals appeared on the scene, particularly organised by the church. It would be interesting to find out more about them. A newspaper report described them as 'an organisation whose right of being is the enjoyment of smoke-pipe musical parties without the usual alcoholic adjuncts'.

The Women's Institute

This national organisation, which was founded in Canada as far back as 1897, reached this country in 1915. A branch started in Stoke Mandeville in 1926 and continues to this day.

A glance at the minute books covering the period of the last war gives a clear insight into what was happening in the village at that time. The Women's Institute was quietly and without fuss organising whist drives, dances, garden parties and many other activities, all with the ultimate aim of raising funds for needy causes both local and national as well as sharing its organisation's expertise in old arts and crafts and learning new ones to aid the war effort. Branches were able to call on its extensive panel of speakers.

At the height of the war, however, some members began to think that charity begins at home and passed a resolution that the branch should not take on the work of raising funds for any new cause however deserving. Obviously too many calls were being made on their limited resources.

Outings also formed part of the institute's activities, but on the whole the war curtailed most of them. Transport was seldom available to go too far afield and speakers often cancelled their visits at short notice when petrol was unavailable.

The Stoke Mandeville banner is something which requires particular mention. A project was afoot in the mid-1930s for each Women's Institute to make a banner, and here in Stoke Mandeville the suggestion was received with enthusiasm. Mrs. Lucy Winterton, the wife of the vicar, was closely involved with the organisation and as a committee member of the Guild of Learners, part of the Produce and Handicraft Guild which until 1972 was a branch of the institute, became the driving force behind the local effort.

Captain William R. W. Kettlewell, R.N. of Westhall Hill, Burford in Oxfordshire was a lecturer for the School of Banners and it was to him that Mrs. Winterton wrote in 1934 as she had attended some of his lectures in Aylesbury asking for his help in designing a banner. She suggested the design should incorporate an historical event connected or linked with the village which was also well known enough by the general public to be of interest. The subject chosen was the Brudenell Tomb and, in particular, the figure of Dorothy which was portrayed on it. After some persuasion Captain Kettlewell became involved and provided the requisite drawings, his only fee being a donation to the Burford

Cottage Hospital of which he was honorary secretary.

Advice was also sought on the appliqué stitching being employed and the type of linen to be used. It seems that old glamis linen was recommended. The Richmond Herald at the College of Arms advised on the Brudenell Arms, Crest and Motto, for the Rev. and Mrs. Winterton were determined to make sure everything was authentic.

The total cost in financial terms was a little over £15, but the time and effort was uncalculable. The Stoke Mandeville ladies carried their finished banner with pride at open air meetings and rallies for many years.

The Ex-Service Men's Association

The Stoke Mandeville Ex-Servicemen's Association was formed immediately after the First World War by homecoming soldiers, who pooled their welfare money and, after many years of additional fund raising, approached the parish council at the end of 1928 to see if they could buy a piece of land on which to build a hall. In their reply the council stated that they had no power to dispose of any such land but an alternative site was subsequently acquired on the west side of the Risborough Road.

37. The original design of the Brudenell banner.

Much of the building work was undertaken by the members themselves, all of whom, under the association's constitution, had to be former servicemen. It was rather a basic building without running water or indoor facilities, water having to be taken from the adjacent standpipe. Between the wars the building was used additionally as a village hall and could be hired at a very competitive rate. It continued to be run by a committee of enthusiastic ex-service men and women and became very lively again after the war. Water and a sewage system were added when the kitchen was enlarged.

Interest began to wane, however, in the late 1950s and, in an effort to boost support, an associate membership was introduced following the death in 1962 of Mr. R. C. Goodram who had served both as secretary and treasurer for many years. The subscription was fixed at 2s. per annum. In 1959 the name of the hall was changed from the Ex-Servicemen's Hall to that of the Memorial Village Hall for Stoke Mandeville.

In 1977 the attention of the parish council was drawn to the bad state of repair of the building and the insanitary conditions inside. The hall had been badly damaged by a storm but no funds were available for repairs. Under the auspices of the Charity Commissioners a sale was arranged, and part of the proceeds formed the enlarged Stoke Mandeville Relief in Need Charity. A new bungalow was built on the site a few years ago.

Stoke Mandeville Twinning

In 1952 Stoke Mandeville was 'twinned' with the Normandy village of Aubigny by the Council of Europe in Strasbourg, who determined the selection of communities. They were usually those of a similar size and situation. Both Aubigny and Stoke Mandeville were considered to be semi-rural, but satellite villages of bigger towns, Aylesbury's equivalent being Falaise. Exchange visits were made each year up to 1959 when they seem to have lapsed. In that year the Stoke party of seven, led by Mr. Ted Luxton of Wendover Road who, with Mr. Vernon, was one of the chief organisers, spent a week with their French hosts visiting a number of local places of interest including the Normandy beaches and Mont-Saint-Michel. This returned the previous year's visit by the French to England.

It was 16 years before the connection was renewed. In 1975 Mr. Luxton and Mrs. Vernon led a small party of seven across the Channel in an effort to revive the 'bond of friendship'. On arriving at Aubigny, the group attended a reception given by the mayor, M. le Marquis d'Aubigny, at his 400-year-old chateau and another later on in the town hall of nearby Falaise, the birthplace of William the Conqueror.

Daily excursions were made to local beauty spots for picnics near lakes, hills and along the Normandy coastline. At the end of the visit, M. le Marquis, mayor for 27 years as his father had been for 30 years before him, said it was one of the best things to have happened to his village. 'But now', he said in faltering English, 'young people should get on with the twinning. We older ones started it and the younger ones should carry it on'.

Meanwhile an approach was made from Mainville seeking cultural links and, in July 1967, 31 pupils and ex-pupils of Stoke Mandeville County Primary School left for a week's trip to the Normandy village which had had historic connections with Stoke Mandeville since 1066. The organisers were Mrs. N. Marshall and Mrs. M. Lake. In 1969 the mayor and mayoress of Mainville, M. and Mme. Leclerc made a return visit with a party of 45 children and parents.

This coincided with the fourth fête organised by the Playing Fields Association.

One question remains unanswered, however. Will these links be recast or have they been broken for ever?

The Stoke Mandeville Society

This short lived organisation was formed in 1973 when wholesale development of the village seemed to threaten the community. In particular the plan to build on a site between Yew Tree House and St Mary's Cottage was strongly opposed, even to the stage of involving the local member of Parliament. Although 179 signatures were collected against the proposed development, this appeal failed, like so many others before and since.

A hundred people attended the inaugural meeting in the Ex-Service Men's Hall. The aims of the Society were to 'try to preserve a village way of life and create a community spirit'. Sixty of those present said they would join, and a steering committee was formed. This society has now sunk without trace.

The Playing Field Association

The possibility of having a playing field for the village does not seem to have been discussed by the parish council from the time Mr. Arnold raised the matter in 1910 until after the Second World War, when the Stoke Mandeville Football Club asked for help in providing one, but no doubt the need for it was often in people's minds. A seven-acre piece of land east of the *Woolpack Inn* had been zoned as an open space under the Town and Country Planning Act of 1937 and enquiries were made about its acquisition, but this came to nothing. A small field close by called Joe's Close was also reserved by the planners.

In 1954 the county council asked if the parish council needed funds for a community centre. They replied that their existing hall was sufficient for their needs but that they would be glad of the provision of a playing field. Two years earlier the secretary of the Bucks. Playing Field Association outlined to a public meeting of interested parties the requirements for playing field facilities essential for every town and village. He also informed the meeting of the procedure and maintenance needed for such a field and what assistance the Bucks. Playing Field Association would give. A generous donation of £50 to start things off came from a local landowner, Mr. Jakobi.

The committee which was formed as a result of this meeting continued to raise funds for a number of years, but it was not until 1965 that a site suitable for its needs was found adjacent to Eskdale Road. The asking price for the three acres was £3,000. A 50 per cent grant came from Buckinghamshire County Council. The parish council gave £900 and the balance was raised by the local Playing Field Association assisted by the Bucks. Playing Field Association.

An annual fête was introduced and this has continued in one form or another with varying levels of support and success to the present day. At the grand opening of the field in 1969 £300 was raised, and in 1974 the various events attracted 1,500 people. Two years later only £250 was taken, 'it being difficult to find people to serve on the committee' – a statement which has a familiar ring to it in the 1990s.

The Community Centre

The Community Association was formed in 1977 following a public meeting during the previous year, when the need for a centre was discussed. The fact was that, although the Ex-Servicemen's Club Hall and to a lesser degree the Parish Room, on the site of the old National school, were available for meetings, neither was suitable for larger functions and it became increasingly obvious that a central community centre was the answer. The hall in particular, by now renamed the Memorial Village Hall, was in a poor state of repair. The Stoke Mandeville Society had conducted a poll of the villagers, which indicated that 85 per cent were in favour of such a centre.

Thanks to the efforts of the parish council, funds were available. At long last the proceeds of the sale of part of the allotments owned by the parish had been received and, after interest had been added, the compensation figure was a little under £100,000.

At the public meeting held in June 1976 at the playing field's pavilion, when 114 of the public attended, plans were laid for the future and a steering committee set up with representatives from all of the organisations in the village. They were drawn from the Playing Field's Committee, the Stoke Mandeville Society, the Women's Institute, the Darby and Joan Club, the Drama Club, the parish council and two members of the public, Messrs. Last and Smithson. Mr. M. Last was elected chairman.

Tenders were soon out and that of Messrs. J. H. Midwinter for £71,000 accepted. The building was completed in 1977 and the grand opening took place on 25 March the following year. Mr. John Paterson, High Sheriff of the county, and Mrs. Paterson, former residents of the parish, cut a two-tier cake topped with a model of the new centre, which had been made by Mrs. Alice Richardson, another local resident. The long cherished dream of many in Stoke Mandeville was fulfilled on this day.

Chapter Twelve

Inns, Shops and Industry

The authorities have sought, through the ages, to control and tax the drink trade, and the licensing of premises started as early as 1552. This was the Act which, amongst other things, restricted opening times during church services. The manor also took an interest in what was going on and its officials reported upon both quality and price as well as measures.

The brewers and publicans had powerful friends in Parliament in the early part of the last century. In 1824 an effort was made to reduce home brewing which had become quite a cottage industry, and under an Act in that year it became illegal to brew and sell liquor anywhere within 100 yards of a public house, and beer could only be consumed on the premises.

A near monopoly then arose, with falling quality and unreasonably high prices. In 1830, however, the burden of licensing was taken out of the hands of the magistrates insofar as beer, ale and cider were concerned, and became the responsibility of the local excise office. Whilst a fee of £30 was payable under the old system, an annual excise licence cost a mere two guineas, amended to one guinea when the Act finally reached the statute book.

This relaxation in the law, and the proposed removal of duty on beer, caused a vast number of retail establishments to spring up. The only requirement, apart from the excise licence and the need to maintain a trouble-free establishment on pain of closure by the Justices in case of 'riot and tumult', was the display of a board in letters 'one inch in length in white upon black or black upon white', bearing the name of the licensee.

Much pressure was put on members of Parliament by those opposed to the new proposals. The brewers' sponsors feared that the quality of beer would fall as the trade, valued at an estimated £20 million per annum, moved from the victuallers to chandlers' shops 'who will adulterate and spoil it'. Those in favour of the changes, however, likened the sale of beer to that of bread and cheese and bacon, 'both necessary for the proper sustenance of a poor man's family'. The object of the bill 'is to enable every poor person, who chooses it, to share a mug of beer with his family at home, which he cannot do at present'. Thus were born 'those abominable places the Beer Houses', as an Aylesbury magistrate termed them in the year of their birth.

Perusal of the records shows that many beer-house keepers combined the sale of beer with their existing occupations, with the wife in charge during the day and the evening session being hosted by the husband. This also applied to the well-established houses before 1830.

And how did all this change affect the parish of Stoke Mandeville? It is thought very little, for all the establishments had been in the village for many decades and certainly well into the previous century. Such places, it seemed, provided a sanctuary for the working man. Miserable and crowded home conditions encouraged men to seek comfort elsewhere. Often the pub was warmer, dryer and probably cleaner than their own cottages, which were filled to overflowing with children of all ages and a harassed, overworked wife.

At the turn of the 18th century, the 1801 census gave the population of Stoke, including the detached portion at Prestwood, as 248. On the basis that three quarters of that figure was women and children, the remaining 60 or so men were served by the five known licensed premises in the parish at that time. These bear the same names as today's houses, the *Bell*, the *Bull* and the *Woolpack*, with the *George* at Prestwood, now a private house, and the defunct *Harrow* at Hall End, but they were undoubtedly very different places from those of today.

It is an interesting fact that, apart from the *Bull*, none of the others is mentioned on the enclosure map of 1798 but, as named premises are on the licensing records, their existence cannot be denied. As has been indicated, there was never a legal requirement to display the name sign of premises. In the isolated villages everyone knew where the inn was without the need for a name and there were few strangers around. It was only when the population became more mobile that names began to be important.

The *Harrow* at Hall End disappeared from the records in 1823 but undoubtedly continued as a beer house until *c.*1860 when it was closed. It had been in the hands of the Smith family from 1760-1804 and at the time of the enclosure, they owned a considerable part of Hall End. Although the building was well built and in reasonable repair, it was demolished by the then owners, the Tappings, in the early part of the Second World War.

The *George* is first mentioned in 1770 and had only two owners from then until 1818. First there was Thomas Owen, his widow, Ann and then William Essex. It closed its doors in 1902 and is now a private house.

The *Bell* appears about the same time and an Edward Heath held the place for 25 years followed by John Ellis for another twenty. Another family who were landlords for more than 30 years were the Benyons or Bennions. Richard Baker and his widow Ann, followed by her son-in-law, Alfred Rae, were there from 1841 to the 1880s. William Bunce was there at the turn of the century. Parts of the present building date from about the middle of the last century and a plaque in the cellar gives the firm date of 1844, but there has been much alteration over the years.

The *Woolpack Inn* first appears in the licensing records in 1790, although there is evidence of premises here with a 'board' as early as 1756. The family of Putnam was associated with the Woolpack for many years and they combined this with their blacksmith shop which stood on the road at right angles to the inn. The final remains of this village smithy, some sheds, were destroyed by fire as recently as 1970. In 1908 the Ancient Monuments Commission reported on the inn, dating the earliest parts as 17th-century with gable and exposed framing, partly thatched but much altered and extended.

Another family connected with the *Woolpack* was that of Bunce. John Bunce first appears as landlord in the middle of the 19th century and he was followed by George until *c.*1908. More recently, from just before the Second World War to *c.*1951, the landlord of the *Woolpack* was Tommy Lucas, the Liverpool and England international soccer star. He first played for Liverpool in 1916 and was in the England squad in 1922, 1924 and 1926. He later managed Ashford.

The *Bull* or *Bull Inn* first appears in 1793 and is the one establishment which is mentioned on the enclosure map, but it was not on the present site. James Fleet was the first licensee but Charles Lucas, the lord of the manor, owned the inn which stood in Swallow Lane, sometimes called Church Lane, approxi-

38. The *Bull Inn*, *c.*1910.

mately where the present Irvine Drive joins the lane. The inn moved to the present site in the last century and, although there is no firm date for this, the only year that a licence was not granted was 1821. It is reasonable therefore to conclude that this is when the move took place, although many alterations have been made over the years. One report states that the building started life as a stable for the cottage next door.

One occupant of the *Bull* who is worth a mention was Emanuel Edwards. In the census of 1841 he was living with his married brother, William, who was the landlord and a shoemaker as indeed was Emanuel. William married Sarah Fleet in 1839 and after, his brother's death in 1846 at the age of 34, Emanuel married his widowed sister-in-law.

In *Leviticus*, chapter 18 verse 16, the faithful were commanded: 'Thou shalt not uncover the nakedness of thy brother's wife', and in verse 29: 'For whosoever shall commit any of these abominations ... shall be cut off from among their people'.

An Act of Parliament in 1907, too late for this particular couple, clarified an obscure position, for after 1835 there was nothing in Common Law to prevent such a union, but a strict interpretation by the Church on grounds of conscience continued, and it was really up to every clergyman to make up his own mind on the matter. The present day Table of Affinity established in 1946 under Canon XCIX omitted this relationship.

So the couple went off to London away from the probing eyes of the village and were married on 5 August 1852 at St Andrew's, Holborn. They had taken lodgings at 1 Norwich Court off Fetter Lane, with Joseph Tyler, a milkman, who incidentally was a witness to the marriage. But the one thing they did wrong, which was probably the cause of the unpleasantness which was to follow, was that Sarah did not reveal that she was a widow but described herself as a spinster. She gave her father's name and occupation as James Edwards, farmer, when he was in fact James Fleet, farmer. But nothing can be hidden for ever and when the couple returned to the village and were seen by all to be living together as man and wife, tongues began to wag.

The parish authorities did everything they could to ostracise them although the attitude of their fellow parishioners is not known. In later years Emanuel rose to serve as parish overseer, but for 30 years the couple were refused Holy Sacrament by succeeding vicars, again on conscientious grounds, although it would seem that they were exceeding their authority in so doing. Had the parties appealed to the bishop, the ban is unlikely to have stood up.

At the end of his life Emanuel had moved to Paddington where he died in 1896, but he was returned to Stoke Mandeville to be buried and lies alongside his wife in the churchyard, she having died 13 years earlier.

William Barrett, an old soldier who served in India where his eldest son was born, held the licence of the *Bull* from 1880 into this century. He topped the poll in the first election for the newly formed parish council in 1894 and was a member for some years. In 1896 he complained about the new rating assessment for the *Bull* which he considered excessive. It seems that the inn had just been rebuilt after being in a dilapidated condition for some years, and had been made smaller – hence the dispute. All three hostelries continue to serve the village.

Within a village community such as Stoke Mandeville there has always been the need for local shops, although the close proximity to the county town of Aylesbury has meant a continuing battle with larger competitors. As access to the town became easier, the labourers' wives tended to shop where the goods were cheaper and the choice greater. On a Saturday evening, after market day, the lanes must have been full of women and children returning home after a day's shopping.

The earliest record of a shop in the village comes from the census of 1851, when the landlord of the *Bull Inn*, Emanuel Edwards, was described as publican and shopkeeper, but what he sold is not known. He was a cordwainer (shoe-maker) by trade. In the 1881 census, a 62-year-old widow, Mrs. Elizabeth Baker,

39. The original village shop at Pond Mead.

40.   Pargeter's corner, *c.*1930.

41.   Starling's stores, *c.*1930.

was running a grocer's shop from Pond Mead on the Risborough Road. William Bunce took over from her and traded until the 1920s. He handed on the business to Mrs. Holloway.

Albert Pargeter's general store was established in 1912 at the crossroads in the centre of the village and later the Stevens family traded from here. Another general store, also selling petrol and home-made ice-cream, was at Ingram Plested's along Station Road. His son Teddy continued this business for many years after his father's death.

William Mason's post office was opened at Fleet Cottage in 1900 and he might well have sold general items as well. He certainly kept a few cows at the back of his cottage. Newspapers and tobacco were sold by the Misses E. and F. Smith from their Station Road premises, and close by was Edwin Smith's farmyard and wheelwright's shop. He was also the local coffin maker and undertaker.

Starling's Stores came somewhat later, as did the butcher's shop in Wendover Road near the Station Road turning. Mr. Prior repaired boots in his cottage at Chapel Row on the Risborough Road, and Mrs. Bailey made boiled sweets in her Swallow Lane cottage as well as selling fireworks in November. These were the retailers in the village in the 1920s and 1930s.

A directory of 1943 shows the picture very little changed and only a few new faces. Goodram's Bridge Poultry Farm had appeared at 59 Station Road as had Mrs. Evans, a poultry breeder, nearby. James Quilter was already established in 1926 with his sausage skin manufacturing factory on the Wendover Road. The sub-post office was at 111 Wendover Road and Prior's boot repairers moved to 42 Station Road. The local police constable lived at 41 Station Road.

The development of industry in the village has been an equally low key affair. It was in 1964 that an application was made by the British Oil and Cake Mills (a subsidiary of Unilever) to set up an experimental pig station at Whitethorne Farm in Old Risborough Road. The parish council opposed it on the grounds of smell and recommended siting it more to the south-west, beyond the parish boundary. How the smell was to be stopped at the boundary was not discussed by the councillors.

Later in the year there was an appeal against this proposed development as well as that for 15 Station Road, where A. N. Saunders & Co. had applied for the premises to be used for the manufacture of cast stone and cement products. The objections were many, but mostly from adjoining neighbours who were worried that they would be permeated with cement dust, 'this being a menace to health'. These premises have subsequently been used as a coach depot by Messrs. Dixon's and currently by Messrs. Mott's Coaches, not without resistance, it must be said, from immediate neighbours.

Chapter Thirteen

A Walk Through 19th-Century Stoke Mandeville

In this chapter an effort will be made, as far as possible, to build up a picture of Stoke Mandeville in the early part of the last century. By using the enclosure map, to which reference has already been made, and comparing it with the 1910 valuation of property, known as the modern Domesday Book, the changes wrought in the century between them can be observed. Where the property can be identified in both documents, the comments of the field valuers are given in brackets.

The first property mentioned at the Aylesbury end of the Lower Road in the 1841 census is Hospital Farm. This has no connection with the present hospital nearby, which started life as the Pest House on the Aylesbury parish boundary. This building became the isolation hospital at the turn of the century and all the development that has taken place since at Stoke Mandeville Hospital has been outside the parish. Hospital Farm was probably an earlier name for Stoke Farm, or Stoke Field Farm as it is called in some records. The Governors of Christ's Hospital leased the great 123-acre Hawkeslade Field on which the farm stood, hence the name of Hospital Farm, although there is no evidence of a building there in 1797.

Bryant's map of 1824-5, however, shows Stoke Field Farm, as does the old series of Ordnance Survey maps which were made at about the same time. Perhaps this was a forerunner of the recently demolished Stoke Farm which was said to have been built around 1850. (1910: a poor place.)

The turning on the right along the Lower Road leads down to Hall End, or All End as it appears in some of the church registers. Although there is only one large cottage there now, much altered and enlarged in the 1930s, the settlement was quite extensive in earlier days, and the population 100 years ago must have totalled 50 souls. There was a public house here called the *Harrow*, mentioned above. There is also a strong possibility that Hall End was the site of one of the two early manors of Stoke Mandeville called Stoke Halling.

Opposite the Hall End turning there were two thatched cottages, which were burnt down one summer evening in June 1930 when a passing steam-driven timber lorry was seen to emit sparks which settled on the straw roof. The combination of hot sun and strong wind quickly gutted the property. An earlier cottage stood on the site in 1797.

Fifty yards nearer the village on the same side of the road there was a tenement divided into two, facing the road end on with, on the far side, a wooden barn roofed with corrugated iron. This barn was thatched until 70 or so years ago. These buildings, together with two small adjoining Victorian cottages, were demolished about twenty years ago and three modern detached houses were erected on the site.

These two dwellings and the barn were mentioned by name on the enclosure award. John Whitchurch's Chapel Cottage had a wheelwright's shop attached and his one-acre Chapel Orchard was on the opposite side of the road. The adjoining cottage with garden was called the Chapel. The barn was said to be the original village chapel and the site occupied by the Victorian cottages was known as Chapel Ground. At the time of enclosure, however, the barn was no longer being used as a chapel. This is known from the Commissioners' report for, in an appeal against the proposed award, the owner stated that '... his house was standing upon ground where a chapel formerly stood and now converted into two tenements'.

42. A cottage on Lower Road, c.1970.

In the early days the Nonconformist or dissenters' chapels were often only the front room of a cottage or part of a barn, as the working class, who formed the bulk of worshippers, had little or no funds. But even so they had to be registered at the Quarter Sessions.

The first Wesleyan Methodist chapel was built on the corner of Chapel Lane in 1815 and rebuilt in 1868. A directory of 1853 notes both a Wesleyan and Primitive Methodist Meeting House in the village, thus confirming the 1851 Return of Religious Houses, when the latter were meeting in the house of William Tapping.

Further along the Lower Road nearer the village stood another cottage that dated from 1797. This was almost certainly the one which was occupied for nearly all her life by Sophie Fenn who, in 1908, aged 91, was the last person to be buried in the churchyard of the old church. The cottage was in a very dilapidated condition at the time of Sophie's death and was pulled down very shortly afterwards. This lady, as the 1881 census reveals, separated from her husband in 1865 and was one of the lacemakers of the village.

Across the road were four cottages, the Bunch Cottages, now a single dwelling and renamed Stoke Cottage about 1974, although it is still known as the Bunch by locals. The next two dwellings shown on the map still exist but are now one cottage called Lone Ash.

Although the present *Bell* is a more recent construction, in the early 19th century there was a collection of small buildings described as 'tenements' on this site, and a licensed house called the *Bell* was operating. By the side of this building was the original lane down to Lower Farm, an earlier name for Moat Farm, although that is now approached from Marsh Lane. Even earlier, for a short while, the same farm went by the name of Brook Close Farm. Parts of this building are the very oldest in the parish. The names of a couple of fields in close proximity were Lane's Close and Brown's Close, and they were both behind the *Bell* site.

43. Cottages on Chapel Ground, *c.*1970.

The present Manor Farm on the east side of Lower Road is about 140 years old, the earlier buildings having been destroyed by fire. This was in the hands of the Lucas family in 1797 who were lords of the manor, although the Commissioners stated at the time that Charles Lucas was insane. His sister succeeded as lady of the manor. Later owners were the Tapping family who had substantial holdings in the village. (1910: Very damp. Several rooms in house have been unoccupied for several years.)

44.   Manor Farm, *c*.1900.

The only other building of note before the crossroads in the centre of the village is reached is Manor Cottage, the present home of Sir William, better known as Dr. William, and Lady Shakespeare.(1910: A nice old house.) This, a modest dwelling at the time of the enclosures, was added to *c*.1924, the name

Manor Cottage being given to it at the turn of the century. There was a large
duck pond outside its back door, hence Pond's Close nearby, and at one time
the house was occupied by one of the old Aylesbury duckers, who earned their
livelihood by the early rearing and fattening of that delicacy in pre-refrigerated
days. Another pair of thatched cottages stood close to the site of the present
village school and they too were burnt down, c.1890.

The farm on the left beyond Manor Farm is ancient, having been recorded
for many years. Although much altered in the 19th century, Malthouse Farm is
of early 17th-century origin. (1910: A nice house.)

45. Cottages in Swallow Lane, c.1908, as romanticised by the Metropolitan Railway.

At the bottom of Swallow Lane, sometimes called in the records Church
Lane, are three small 'one up and one down' cottages in an L shape. Although
much altered in Victorian times, these still remain as a thatched cottage, Willow
Thatch, while the other two are now one dwelling, Swallow Cottage. (1910:
Rental 2s. 6d. per week.) The Royal Commission on Historical Monuments,
commenting on these properties in 1912, stated that 'one wing of the block has
two walls of 17th-century brick and timber and the end wall is of late 17th-cen-
tury blue and red bricks; the other wing is almost entirely modern'.

Three tiny cottages on the east side of the lane are now one property, Clover Cottage. Although there were four cottages here at one time, one was demolished at the time of the conversion. Two more properties shown on the map, which were pulled down in the mid-1960s when Irvine Drive was developed, were the buildings which housed the earlier *Bull Inn*, which moved to its present site on the Risborough Road *c.*1821, and Swallow Lane Farm House. (1910: A nice house.)

Station Road, as it is known today, is relatively new (indeed it bore the name New Road for some while), and was a track connecting the two 'main' roads. It was not until the railway came to the village in 1892 that any significant development took place, and even as late as 1910 there were very few dwellings along it.

Earlier mention has been made of the Old Parsonage which stood well back in Marsh Lane, then Blesbury (Blessbury in some records) Lane. On the site of Mr. King's bungalow, Elm Cottage in Marsh Lane, stood a much earlier building which is clearly shown on the map. All the land west of the brook was in Elles-

46. Silverbrook, in Marsh Lane, *c.*1930.

borough parish and so Brook Cottage, formerly Brook Farm, is not shown. The parish boundary at this point has undergone several changes over the years.

Returning to the centre of the village, Oak Tree House was built *c.*1850, replacing the original old farmhouse which stood close by. The farm buildings survived until the 1920s. (1910: Farm buildings very old indeed and in dilapidated condition.) The new house stood further back from its present frontage as the Risborough Road was realigned to the west in the 1930s. It had a very large orchard which stretched all the way to the next farm, Yew Tree Farm. Close by was Fleet Cottage, which in later years housed the village post office. At the time of enclosure this cottage was occupied by a Mr. Ashwell Christmas. Before the road was altered, the cottage was reached by a long path.

The next building is that of St Mary's Cottage, which was once two dwellings. The front one nearest the main road is said to date from the 15th century, and is of a 'cruck' design. Two great wooden beams providing the framework of the house arc from the ground and meet at the apex of the roof, but the daub and plaster walls have been bricked over. The back cottage, which is a century younger, has a post and truss timber framework. The building was used a restaurant *cum* tea shop during and after the Second World War and went by the delightful name of Cookery Nook.

47. Cookery Nook, now St Mary's cottage.

Freehold ESTATE,

TITHE-FREE and INCLOSED;

TO BE SOLD BY AUCTION,

At the *White Hart Inn* at AYLESBURY;

On SATURDAY the 3d. Day of MARCH, 1804,

AT FOUR O'CLOCK IN THE AFTERNOON;

A Compact Estate,

Situated at *Stoke Mandeville*, in the County of *Buckingham*,

In the Occupation of Mr. GREEN, Tenant at Will,

Consisting of a Farm House, Stable, Cowhouse, two Barns and other convenient Buildings, with the following Parcels of rich Pasture and Arable Land.

	A.	*R.*	*P.*
The Homestall and Home Ground, *Pasture,*	5	0	19
The Close and Paddock, - - - *Pasture,*	9	3	4
The new Allotment on the Green, *Pasture,*	0	3	31
Ditto, - - - - in West Field, *Arable,*	19	2	37
Total,	35	2	11

It is well situate for Markets, being within three Miles both of *Aylesbury* and *Wendover.*

For a View of the Estate, apply to the Tenant, and for Particulars, to Mr. DAVIS, Land Surveyor, of *Lewknor*, OXON. or *Holiwell*, OXFORD.

48. Whitethorn Farm auction details, 1804.

Yew Tree House, a little further along, is another ancient farmhouse which, when viewed from the rear, indicates a splendid mixture of periods and styles and certainly dates back to the 16th century, while the eastern block was rebuilt in 1716. (1910: A very nice house.)

The Wesleyan Methodist chapel was built on the corner of Chapel Lane in 1815, too late to be shown on the map. It was rebuilt about fifty years later and ceased to be a place of worship in 1958, when new premises were found in Eskdale Road. Where Chapel Lane is now, a track led up to a row of cottages close to the old farm buildings belonging to Yew Tree Farm. Nearby was a property known as Armlases Farm which was very ancient. First mentioned in 1630, it formed part of the marriage settlement of Henry Smith, but was demolished c.1885. (1910: Court Farm, building and agricultural land near Chapel Lane owned by Sir Oswald Mosley now demolished.)

Beyond the vicarage site along the Risborough Road (1910: Some very bad settlement) is the *Belmore Hotel*, which was formerly Whitethorne House, the home of the Gurney family and later of Sir Oswald Mosley. An earlier building on or near this site appears on the enclosure map and an auction of this property took place in 1804.

49.   Stoke House, *c.*1910, before the new wing was added.

On the other side of the road a drive leads up to Stoke House, in 1797 noted as a homestead, yard and orchard, certainly smaller than today. The Royal Commission on Ancient Monuments describes it as early 18th-century, altered and extended in similar style in 1922. Before the new wing was constructed, the main entrance was on the south-west side of the house. On the left of the drive stands the building housing the now sadly ruinous mill wheel. The old church stood 250 yards to the south-east.

Returning towards the centre of the village, in 1797 there was a garden in the hands of Richard Olliffe on the site of the present Ivy Lea. By the time of the corn rent assessment in 1841, however, a cottage had been built here belonging to the parish, the Parish House. The present building, which has been enlarged, was built as the schoolmaster's house in the 1880s at the expense of the then vicar. (1910: Rental 3s. per week.) Directly next door, at a slight angle to the road, stands Pond Mead which, in the middle of the century, was the village's original grocer's shop.

Nearby was Pondmead Homestead, which by the beginning of the century had degenerated into a pair of dilapidated thatched cottages. One of these was

50.   Pond Mead Homestead, *c*.1930.

unoccupied for some years before the last World War but in the other lived a retired octogenarian bachelor shepherd, Frank Grace, who was the last person in the parish to wear the traditional Buckinghamshire farm worker's lace smock. (1910: One up and one down. Estimated annual rental £3 per annum as part of wages.) On the evening of 21 June 1940, freak lightning struck the cottages and although there was very little accompanying rain they were soon destroyed, but not before Frank had time to throw quite a number of gold sovereigns from an upstairs window to a small crowd which quickly gathered on the scene.

The site of the present Burgoyne and Spencer Cottages was in 1797 occupied by cottage dwellings. At the beginning of the century there were five small cottages here and, on a map accompanying a sale catalogue of Stoke House in 1911, the larger one at the north end of the five is described as a Methodist chapel. The rent of these in the early 1900s was 1s. 6d. inclusive. As has been said, the Wesleyan chapel was rebuilt in 1868 on the corner of Chapel Lane to replace an earlier one. It is not clear whether this end cottage was in fact the original site, or the map was drawn wrongly.

The *Woolpack Inn*, next in this walk back into the past, was only a cottage in 1797 but, as has been seen. the inns of the village were often quite modest affairs and, from the licensing records, it is certain that the inn, in one form or other, was in the village well before enclosure. The building has 17th-century origins, timber-framed with brick and plaster filling, and it was restored in the last century. There is some exposed framing in the gable end, while half of the roof is thatched and the other half tiled. The wooden building, which stood at right angles to the main one, was the village smithy for many decades, Holloway and Eldridge being but two names associated with it. Although it had long ceased to be used as a smithy, the remaining sheds on the site were destroyed by fire in the 1970s.

Next to the *Bull Inn*, which formerly stood in Swallow Lane and was moved to its present site in the 1820s, are three cottages which at the time of the enclosure award can be identified as a 1½-acre Homestead and Home Close. This is the property on which Jackson's Charity was established in 1726. In that year John Jackson, who was lord of the manor, in carrying out the wishes of his father, Thomas Jackson, established a yearly rent charge of £1 on the cottages to be spent on the provision of 120 twopenny loaves of good wholesome bread for the poor of Stoke Mandeville. Bread rationing after the war changed the gift to that of money, and this continues to the present day. (1910: Rent 1s. 6d. per week each, increased to 2s. 6d. after improvements.)

The last cottage to be looked at in this walk through 19th-century Stoke Mandeville is the one next door to the *Bull Inn*, now called Ye Old Thatched Cottage, a name it has had for at least 70 years. It is believed to have been called Crickmans at one time. This 'Cottage and Garden' is said to be one of the oldest in the village although it is rather difficult to distinguish fact from legend. Said by the Royal Commission on Historic Monuments to be 17th-century, others claim it dates from the 15th. Within the cottage there is a slab inset into the floor with the date 1409.

The place is said to have had connections with the Boleyn family, hence the legend that it was the home of Anne Boleyn, who has been called the 'Fair Maid of Aylesbury'. Certainly her father, the Earl of Salisbury, better known by his earlier title of Sir Thomas Bullen, inherited the town of Aylesbury through his mother in 1529, and Anne must have lived at the Manor House in Kingsbury from time to time. How the legend arose that King Henry came 'a calling' is not clear. A recent owner stated that there are two stained-glass windows on the south side of the cottage depicting Henry and Anne, but they appear to be Victorian.

51. Yew Tree Farm barns, c.1970.

As this walk through 19th-century Stoke Mandeville finishes on this corner, for there were no buildings along Station Road until the end of the century, it is worth mentioning the ancient barns which still exist in the village, older than many of the other buildings under review. Since the destruction of the barns at Yew Tree Farm some 25 years ago to make way for the modern development close by, there remain but two. They are the tall barn with the sharply pitched roof which stands to the right of Malt House Farm and a similar, but somewhat larger one, at Old Moat Farm off Marsh Lane.

They were once threshing barns and although they now have corrugated iron roofs, originally they would have been tiled or thatched. The one at Moat Farm, however, is unique in the district as it had the original Mowstead (pronounced-Muse-ted) in the central aisle. This consisted of a high wooden platform with sides about three feet high, on which grain was threshed with a flail – two pieces of wood, one a handstake about three and a half feet long, and a swingel about a foot shorter. The swingel was attached by a leather thong to a swivel on the handstake, and was whirled around to thresh the ears of grain out of the sheaves.

52.   The interior of Moat Farm barn.

This type of work, which was carried out under cover in the barns, provided winter employment for the farm workers where none would otherwise have been available. This all ceased when machinery was introduced and the threshing machines took over, completing the job in hours.

An indication of how the village was developing 100 years later is found in a valuation of property made for tax purposes in 1910. A detailed map was produced at the same time. Before the days of the owner occupier most property was rented, and it is interesting to note how many landlords in the return were living outside the village.

The chief landowners were John Henry Tapping, who was also lord of the manor, Lord Rothschild, Frederick Whitchurch on the Isle of Wight, the trustees of Jeffery Gadsden of Weston Turville and the trustees of Richard Gurney of Saunderton. In addition there were a number of other absent land-lords who owned three or four cottages each, and whilst their rental income was relatively small, no doubt repairs and maintenance were also kept to a mini-mum.

In the mid-1920s development of the centre of the village began to accelerate and, in particular, of the plots on the right-hand side along Station Road. In a list of voters in 1918 those on the north side of the road were limited to:

Albert Pargeter – Bushey Cottage. Miss Wheeler – Rose Cottage. Joseph Timms and Charles Kidnee – Rose Cottages. Joseph Stilton – The Homestead. William Honour – The Firs. Alfred Skinner – Grove Bungalow. Edwin Smith's – Black-smith's yard. Mrs. Lendon – The Cot. Fred Lee – The Limes.

There were no more houses from here up to the Wendover Road, apart from Ferndale (no. 47) and on the south side nothing apart from Milton Bungalow, Coronation Cottages and the Smiths until those beyond the railway bridge. Westwood (no. 56) and two or three bungalows completed the picture. By 1926, however, there had been a remarkable change in a short time. Seven properties had been built between the Station Bridge and the Wendover Road, and a further 10 up to Ferndale. On the other side, four or five bungalow plots beyond the station were occupied and another 10 or so houses had been built nearer Pargeter's Corner, including the shop itself. In addition 20 council houses had sprung up at the junction with what is now Hampden Road.

The population of Stoke Mandeville remained more or less stable for 100 years between 1811 and 1911 at around 450 souls, although boundary changes and a different method of calculation have made absolute comparisons difficult, and there was a dip at the turn of the century. Up to the middle of the last cen-tury, the population was rising steadily and by 1851 was at a peak of 538, having doubled in 50 years. With Prestwood out of the figures and deep agricultural depression encouraging a drift from the country to towns and overseas, a low of 282 was recorded in 1901.

Then, with the building boom of the '20s and '30s, a figure of 606 was reached in 1931, doubling in two decades. With the continuing growth of the housing estates to the north of the parish with Aylesbury postal addresses, the figure rose to 3,678 and undoubtedly, when the result of the 1991 census is known, a further increase can be expected.

Chapter Fourteen

Some Outstanding Characters in the Village

Christopher Edward ARNOLD (1849-1923)

This gentleman came from Yardley Hastings National School for Boys in Northamptonshire in 1893 to become the first headmaster of the Stoke Mande-

53. Christopher E. Arnold, *c.*1905, the first headmaster.

ville board school. He soon established himself as an outstanding teacher and played a full part in the life of the community serving as parish clerk and assistant overseer of the poor for many years.

He lived some while at the schoolmaster's house opposite the vicarage in Risborough Road but later, due to problems with the then vicar and the poor condition of the house, moved to the New House, Moat Farm (now the home of Mr. Richard Pearce). His wife, Eliza, assisted as sewing mistress and both of his daughters, Edith and Margaret, were for a time teachers at his school. Edith died in 1921 but her mother lived on until 1936.

Margaret married Mr. Samuel G. Johnson of Hunt Barnard & Co. in 1909. They continued to live at the New House with her parents during the First World War but then moved to Bushey Cottage on the corner of Swallow Lane and Station Road. The garden of this house was much larger than

106

it is now. Complete with tennis court and stabling it was one of the most sought-after villas in the village.

Fanny Mary Fleet BONEST (1841-1911)

This lady was the daughter of William and Sarah Edwards née Fleet, who were the landlords of the *Bull Inn*, and her step-father was Emanuel Edwards, the parish overseer who later farmed Swallow Lane Farm.

In 1888 she married a local butcher, William Turpin Young, but early the next year he met with a fatal accident. When returning from Tring market on a dark February evening, he drove his cart off the road near Halton and it over-turned in the brook where his body was found by the passing mail carrier. He had called at the *Rose and Crown* at Tring on his way home, the landlord reported, but he was sober when he left. He had also been seen in the *New Inn* at Buckland the same afternoon. History was to repeat itself seven years later when his brother-in-law, Thomas Fleet Edwards, was found drowned in a ditch.

The following year she married a wealthy 71-year-old gentleman farmer, William Bonest of Manor Farm, Mentmore, who also farmed land in Stoke Man-deville. He died in 1891 in London, and he left £500 in his will to his new wife. Upon her husband's death she returned to Stoke Mandeville and took up residence at Bushey Cottage.

Mrs. Bonest died there in 1911 and is buried in the churchyard where the death of her nephew, William Emanuel Edwards, is also recorded. He was killed in action at High Wood on the Somme and was the son of Joseph Emanuel Edwards and Mary Martha Tapping who, in 1881, were farming Brook Cottage and its 12 acres. In 1895 Joseph was farming Timms Farm and was an assistant overseer for the parish, in no small measure due to the influence of his brother-in-law, John Henry Tapping.

THE GURNEYS

Thomas Gurney, a gentleman farmer, lived at Whitethorne House and farmed this estate from the early part of the last century until his death in 1862. His generosity to the parish included a gift of land where both the vicarage and the National school stood. His other claim to fame was that his son-in-law was Robert Gibbs, the proprietor of the *Bucks Advertiser and Aylesbury News*, and the author of the *History of Aylesbury* and other works of local interest.

Thomas Gurney, a surgeon and a widower, was living at Oak Tree House in 1871, and it was he who was mentioned in the divorce suit between the Rev. Charles Partington and his wife. He was the younger son of Thomas Gurney of Whitethorne, and as a boy of six laid the foundation stone of the National school in 1844.

Gurney's Farm, which is shown on early maps of this century, along the Lower Road, acquired the name of the Red House *c.*1913 when the rental was

54. Mr. John Irvine.

£12 per annum. The trustees of the Gurney estate were then the owners.

John IRVINE (1883-1969)

Mr. Irvine was first elected to the parish council in 1945 and served several times as chairman. He was also on the rural district council for 10 years. Born in Cramond near Edinburgh, he went to sea at 16 and served his apprenticeship in sailing ships. He obtained his Master's Certificate in steam in 1907, having twice gone round Cape Horn. He was commissioned in the R.N.V.R. during the First World War and settled in Stoke Mandeville when hostilities ceased.

Apart from his work as a councillor, he interested himself in the Playing Field Association, the Ex-Service Men's Club and the Stoke Mandeville Garden and Allotment Society.

William Nanson LETTSOM (1796-1865)

This gentleman, although not a resident, was one of Stoke Mandeville's landowners in the mid-1800s and owned the land on which the new church was built. He was the eldest grandson of Dr. J. C. Lettsom, a Quaker physician of considerable literary repute and friend of the prison reformer James Neild.

William Lettsom himself is described as a man of letters and, after Eton and Trinity College, Cambridge, where in 1816 he won the prizes for the Latin ode and two epigrams, devoted his life to a study of literature, both ancient and modern. How he came to own property in Buckinghamshire is not clear, nor if, or how often, he visited it, but his donation of land adjacent to Malt House Green made the new church possible. He also donated £75 towards the cost of the building.

When the church was consecrated 10 months after Lettsom's death, a fitting tribute to his generosity was made by the vicar of the parish, Charles Partington. At the celebratory luncheon, Mr. Partington said that he '... was never applied to for aid in any good work without effect. When asked for a site [for the church], he said, "If there is no portion of my land which is suitable, choose a piece with the most central position, and whatever it costs, I will give it: you are asking me to bring a blessing on the rest of my land" '.

Edward Faux MORRIS (1868-1971)

Mr. Morris was born at Bedgrove Farm but, in the great agricultural depression of 1879, his father sold the property to the first Lord Rothschild of Tring Park. Edward Morris, with his brother, owned the Walton Foundry for 40 years and came to live at Yaxley Lodge at 190 Wendover Road *c.*1930, his father having built the property some years earlier.

On his 100th birthday he told the press that he still mowed the lawn on his three-acre garden by hand: 'I had a motor mower but it was too fast for me'. Upon his move to Coombe Close in May 1968, his housekeeper, Miss. M. Littlefair, said of him: 'He still has a good memory and is wonderful at business. It is only his hearing that is not too good. He used to do a lot of gardening and he misses that'.

An active member of the Aylesbury Rifle Club until he was 90, Mr Morris died aged 103 on 12 October 1971.

55. Mr. Edward F. Morris.

Sir Oswald MOSLEY (1848-1915)

This gentleman, grandfather of the politician of the same name who became notorious as the leader of the British Union Party in the 1930s, owned extensive property in the village. Whitethorn, described as a 'Pleasure Farm with Villa Residence, Farm Building and Yard and 32 Acres' went up for auction in June 1879. It was further advertised as

> Country Retreat being three miles from the London & North Western and Great Western Railway Stations at Aylesbury and the same distance from the Great Western Railway at Little Kimble. It is also well adapted as a Hunting Box being in the immediate neighbourhood of Baron Rothschild's Stag Hounds, the Old Berkeley Fox Hounds, the 'Berkhampstead' Buck Hounds and several other packs.

Auction agents even 100 years ago knew how to bring out the best in their advertisements.

Apart from the vicarage site, practically the whole of the west side of the Risborough Road from Chapel Lane to Whitethorns, including the cottages in Chapel Lane and an adjacent farm now defunct called Court Farm, was part of the estate which Mosley purchased in about 1898. By 1910 this farm has been demolished, although the barns remained for some years. A name linked with him at this date, and resident at Whitethorns, was a Miss Florence Freebourn.

His grandson, Oswald Ernald Mosley, whilst a boy, is said to have spent his holidays at Whitethorns. His own parents were, by this time, separated and his

THE FREEHOLD
ESTATE OF "WHITETHORN"

COMPRESS

32½ ACRES,

MORE OR LESS,

IN THE FOLLOWING ENCLOSURES—
IN STOKE MANDEVILLE.

NO.			A.	R.	P.
3	Bow Mead, Pasture				
4	The Ground, ,,				
5	Cages, ,,				
6	Barnes Piece, ,,		15	1	11
7	The Orchard, ,,				
8	Homesteads, ,,				
9	House and Garden				

IN ELLESBOROUGH.

1	Home Field, Arable		9	0	39
2	The Pits, Pasture		7	3	30
	Total		32	2	0

"WHITETHORN"

Is prettily situate at the South end of the Village of Stoke Mandeville; is bounded on the South by the High Road from Aylesbury to Wycombe, on the West by the Estate of the Baron L. de Rothschild, and on the North and East by "Ford's" Property; is well watered by a Stream rising at the foot of the Chiltern Hills.

THE FARM BUILDINGS AND YARD

Are contiguous to the House; are commodious and well arranged.

THE RESIDENCE,

Which stands a short distance from the High Road, contains Entrance Hall, Drawing Room, Dining Room, Five Bedrooms, One Attic, Front and Back Kitchens, Store Room, Cellarage, Dairy, W. C.; is modern, conveniently arranged, and substantially built. There are the usual Out-Offices. Adjoining is a KITCHEN GARDEN and ORCHARD, and the LAWN in Front is tastefully Planned. The Aspect is good.

The Lot is very desirable as a Country Retreat, being about three miles from the London and North-Western and Great Western Railway Stations at Aylesbury, and the same distance from the Great Western Station at Little Kimble. It is also well adapted as a Hunting Box, being in the immediate neighbourhood of Baron Rothschild's Stag Hounds, the Old Berkeley Fox Hounds, the Berkhampstead Buck Hounds, and several other Packs.

The Property will be sold subject to an Annuity of £45 per Annum, payable during the life of a gentleman aged 62, and to the payment of £874 1s. 11d. upon the determination of the Annuity at his decease.

The Timber and a Granary have been valued at £　　　, and will have to be paid for by the Purchaser at such sum.

56.　Whitethorn Farm auction details, 1879.

grandfather took a great deal of interest in him. His close relationship with his mother and grandfather, who both adulated him, remained a strong influence with him until their respective deaths.

Edward 'Teddy' James PLESTED (1904-1987)

Mr. Plested was well known in the village as the proprietor of the stores in Station Road, and was particularly famous for his ice-cream, the secret recipe being known only to the family. His father, Ingram, first sold it from an old Darracq car which was equipped with acetylene headlights. When Teddy acquired a motor cycle, his father bought him a sidecar from which to sell the ice-cream, and he became a familiar figure outside schools, at fairs and at other local events. At its peak the round took him seven miles from the village and eventually the business was served by two motorcycle combinations and two pedal cycles with ice-cream boxes attached.

57. Teddy Plested.

Former pupils of Stoke Mandeville school well remember how, at the end of every season, he would go down to the school where the children would be lined up ready and waiting to receive a free ice-cream. As time went by, he was serving the children of those whom he had served as children themselves. The shop closed in 1969, only the garage remaining. A small housing estate now stands on the site with only the name, Plested Court, reminding us of Teddy.

THE SMITHS

Edwin Smith's wheelwright shop and house, with its farm-yard, was in Station Road. The workshop stood where the present Mott's Coaches (formerly Dixon's) are housed, and he lived in the cottage opposite. Mr. Smith was also for a time the village undertaker, and one of his rooms, normally the parlour, was used for laying-out when clients were in residence.

George, his son, who had served for two years in the Royal Engineers during the First World War, was killed in an accident in February 1943. He was bringing a two-ton load of timber from St Leonards when the brakes of the lorry failed.

58. Edwin Smith.

The inquest revealed that the driver was having difficulty with the gears and to avoid it running away down the hill, he drove the lorry into some railings to halt it. Whether George jumped out, thinking the vehicle was out of control, or was thrown out upon impact is not clear, but he was found dead near the lorry.

Miss Ethel Smith was a familiar figure on her paper round. She collected the newspapers from the station in her battered pram and delivered them throughout the village in all weathers.

Edwin Smith lived on in his old age as a rather cantankerous figure, bossing everyone in sight, and giving his daughter, with whom he lived, quite a hard time. He died in 1938 and, although he was buried in St Mary's churchyard, there is no tombstone to mark the spot. He is supposed to have said that 'e didn't want no stone over is head cause he might not be able to push to is way hup when that there trumphet sounded'.

THE TAPPINGS

The Tappings have been farmers and landowners in Stoke Mandeville for at least 200 years. In the 1851 census William Tapping (1789-1853) farmed from the Manor House and 30 years later his grandson, John Henry, employed 16 workers at the same farm (six men, six boys and four ploughmen). His own father, William, who farmed there before him, died in 1862 at the relatively early age of 43, and his widow, Mary, carried on for many years with the help of her sons. She died in 1904.

In spite of the agricultural depression at the turn of the century, the family seems to have managed very well to keep going, and by 1910, at the time of the tax survey, John Henry was the lord of the manor. The Lucas family held the manor for 100 years before this.

In the same return the extent of the Tappings' holdings is revealed. In addition to Manor Farm, which son William farmed, they owned property and land at Hall End, Malt House Farm and the wheelwright's shop and house in Station Road, as well as tied farmworkers' cottages scattered around the village. Malt House Farm and its 38 acres was bought at auction in June 1908 for £1,789 from the Bennett family. Stoke House was also put up for auction at the same time, the Tappings having lived there since at least 1891.

At the time of his death in 1921, John Henry Tapping owned almost 2,000 acres in the Vale of Aylesbury, not only in Stoke parish but also large farms at Quainton, Rowsham and Weston Turville. Bedgrove Farm, then in the latter parish, was a fine Georgian house and was Mr. Tapping's home for many years. This in turn was occupied and farmed by one of his sons, Henry, until its demolition in the 1960s to make way for the Bedgrove housing estate.

Freddy FOSTER (1865-1939)
As a finale to the solid and respectable citizens of Stoke Mandeville whose lives have been outlined in the last few pages of this history, we conclude the chapter and the book by way of complete contrast with that of an individual well known to older villagers between the Wars, who in his youth was undoubtedly a most accomplished sportsman, but in later years became a popular and likeable alcoholic.

Freddy was born in a cottage at Stoke Farm (long since demolished) where his father was farm bailiff. In his youth he became on the cricket field a bowler of outstanding ability. This came to the notice of the College authorities at Eton and Freddy was employed there around the 1890s as a cricket coach and groundsman. In this capacity he represented Buckinghamshire for many years, but, in view of his employment as a school cricket coach, he was considered a professional and was always put down on the score sheet by his surname only, whilst almost all the other players who were 'gentlemen' had initials in front of their names.

Unfortunately, however, Freddy became increasingly addicted to strong liquid refreshment and, his playing days over, he returned to agricultural work in the village. Thanks to his habitual intemperance he had no regular employer, but was used as a seasonal helper by local farmers.

His addiction was not helped in the early part of the century by the young Oswald Mosley (whose name appears earlier in this chapter) who found it amusing to ply him with large quantities of drink in the local hostelries. No matter how much beer Freddy had consumed, once he managed to mount his penny-farthing bicycle he could always ride home along Lower Road into Stoke Farm Lane, now Kynaston Avenue, towards the railway line. Halfway along there was a steep drop, and then a rise up to the crossing gates which were always shut. Unable to stop, the penny- farthing would deposit him over the gates and there he would lie until he was sober, with no late night trains to disturb his drunken stupor. He spent his last days in a caravan, in a field near the station, by courtesy of William Tapping.

The Partington Affair – A Vicar's Petition for Divorce

On Thursday 29 February 1872, the vicar of Stoke Mandeville petitioned for divorce on the grounds of his wife's adultery. The suit was extensively reported in the press, and the bulk of the following has been taken from these reports and those of the two subsequent trials for perjury after the divorce case.

The Rev. Charles Edward Partington was Stoke Mandeville's first vicar, and the parish must be grateful for his guiding hand during the building of the new church. As has been seen, Stoke had been a chaplaincy of Bierton and the curate there was in charge until 1858. What drew Mr. Partington away from Lancashire, the county of his birth, will never be known but he was married at Twickenham parish church on 6 December 1859. His bride was Miss Myfanwy Jane Kerr, aged 18, from Llangollen in Wales and 15 years his junior.

By 1866 three children had been born, but after the birth of the last child, Ernest Edward, in May 1866, Dr. Warren was reported as saying that if she ever had another child she would die. Mrs. Partington acted as church organist, attending the services on Sunday as well as playing for the choir practice in the vestry for an hour or so on weekdays.

It was in the autumn of 1870 that an 18-year-old youth named Frederick James Townend appeared on the scene. He was studying for orders and staying 'for the benefit of his health' at Oak Tree House, the home of a surgeon, Mr. Thomas Gurney. It was not long before Mr. Townend, with the vicar's permission, was helping with the music, as his wife was so often unwell that she could not always attend to her musical duties. After choir practice, the young couple were in the habit of remaining in the vestry and playing over the music for Sunday's service as there was only one chant book. But only once did they remain alone after the main practice, for more than 20 minutes, and then Eliza Daniels, her 32-year-old maid from Stone, came to take Mrs. Partington home.

It was not long before the village was buzzing with rumours about what might or might not be happening in the vestry. The vicar does not appear to have been over popular with some of his flock. There was disagreement concerning the form of some of the music and the vicar had banned one of his parishioners from the sacrament.

On the evening of 11 January 1871, when the choir practice was over, the couple were left on their own. Whilst Frederick was writing out the music for the next evening, Mrs. Partington looked up and saw faces at the window which she knew to be those of local boys well known to her. Mr. Townend went out and spoke to them, and soon after he left the vestry with Mrs. Partington. As they did so there was a further altercation with the boys.

On Friday 24 February a letter arrived at the vicarage from the churchwardens advising Mr. Partington of the rumours circulating in the parish respecting misconduct between his wife and Townend. He handed it to his wife who, after reading it, said, 'Charles. Do you believe it?', to which he replied, 'No, wife, I do not'. Then she said, 'On my solemn oath, there is not one word of truth in it', and advised him to prosecute the boys who had spread the lie. As they parted, Partington kissed his wife, the first time he had done so for several years. They had ceased sleeping together five years earlier during her last confinement. Mr. Partington wrote to the churchwardens expressing disbelief in the aspersions cast upon her but subsequently, after investigations, instituted the suit against his wife.

At the trial, which took place in August 1872, the principal witnesses for the prosecution were the two lads, who swore that they had seen through the vestry window acts of adultery on many occasions and once between the respondent and Dr. Gurney, as well as hearing language of the most gross kind between the parties. Myfanwy Partington denied the charges most firmly. She had not committed adultery with Townend either in the vestry or anywhere else. Nor had she called him Ned or Neddie, and he always addressed her as Mrs. Partington.

Townend also denied the charges. He stated that the village boys were in the habit of annoying them by looking in at the vestry window, but no complaint had been made of the matter either to the magistrate or to the police in the neighbourhood.

Under cross examination he agreed he had put a book over a crevice in the window but had done it to give the boys peering in a little more trouble for their inquisitiveness. Upon being asked if he did not know that he had very seriously compromised the lady, he explained that he thought that if he discontinued the practice that would be tacit admission of guilt on his part. He also said that the reason he and Mrs. Partington did not leave the premises at the same time as the choir was because they did not choose to do it. He also testified that he was away from Stoke Mandeville upon one occasion when it was said that he had acted improperly.

There was an arrangement that if they were insulted again the church bell was to be rung once and Dr. Gurney would come to their assistance and escort her home, which he did. (The Doctor's property Oak Tree House still stands almost opposite the church.) Townend agreed that Mrs. Partington had lent him novels to read on several occasions but he did not remember the names of the books. They were not 'love' novels more than any other books. No, he had never thought of going to the vicar to assure him that there was no foundation for the charges which he agreed had been circulating in the village concerning his supposed intimacy with Mrs. Partington.

Dr. Gurney, in his turn, denied that any impropriety had ever occurred between him and Mrs. Partington. He acknowledged having received a letter from the vicar requesting him to cease visiting the house, as indeed had Townend, alluding to 'painful circumstances' and asking him not to come again to his church. Up to that time both he and his wife had been on terms of intimacy as neighbours for 14 years. Any gifts he had given Mrs. Partington after his wife's death were in deference to the express wish of Mrs. Gurney during her lifetime. He had always treated Mrs. Partington as a sister.

On the third day the jury stopped the case saying that they had heard enough to convince them that they did not believe the story told by the two village boys, and the respondent and co- respondent were found not guilty of adultery. The subsequent trials of the two main witnesses took place at the Central Criminal Court and, in spite of a number of local people acting as character witnesses in both cases, they were sentenced to terms of two years and 18 months hard labour respectively.

Village opinion was outraged. Those who knew the lads best said they could not have committed the serious offences, and one of the defending counsels at the trial was probably very near the truth when he said that his clients genuinely thought they saw something which was perhaps worse than it really was.

The boys served out their sentences and on 4 June 1874 the village celebrated their return. As the date drew near for the second release, a subscription list was started and this was headed by Lord Rothschild's agent. Many helped to swell the fund and, as was said later at the presentation, 'all ranks and classes in the village subscribed towards the proceedings of that day, not only those comparatively well off, but many poor men and women contributed and that it was thought as much of the poor man's sixpence as of the rich man's sovereign'.

A large crowd gathered at the Aylesbury London and North Western railway station to welcome home one of the youths, and plans were afoot to draw the trap which was to collect him from the station the last part of the journey by hand. (It was common practice at that time to take the horse out of the shafts and for friends to pull the conveyance as an act of welcome.) But the plan misfired when the young man slipped unheralded into Stoke Mandeville by another route.

The homecoming celebrations continued, however, and a marquee was erected on one of the fields belonging to his widowed mother where 'an abundant cold collation was laid out and partaken by a numerous assemblage'. During the subsequent speeches mention was made of the fact that the village was still without a clergyman – Partington having resigned the living – which was a great inconvenience and a loss, and all trusted that they would soon have one amongst them with whom they would be able to work.

More speeches followed and healths of the guests of honour were drunk with the comment that all present had known the lads from boyhood and never known them tell a lie, an obvious reference to the charges of perjury. At long last the presentations of pocket watches were made to the boys and, in turn, each made a speech in reply. The elder boy said that he was much obliged for all their kindness and the way in which the presentation had been made. The other said that as it had been a long time since he had been allowed to use his voice freely, they should not expect him to say very much. He then went on to say quite a lot.

He said he would always value the watch and trusted they would always find him worthy of the esteem which had been expressed towards him now he was once more amongst them. He was sorry that there was no clergyman there and, for his part, he would always be very pleased, when they had one again in the village, to do everything he could to assist and support him in any good work for the welfare of the parish. He was very grateful for the sympathy of his friends, which would long rest in his memory, and he trusted that such an occurrence would never happen again, not only for his sake but for that of his kind friends and neighbours.

John Henry Tapping went on to become a highly successful farmer, a respected and leading member of the community and chairman of both the parish council and a governor of the Board School before his death at Bedgrove Farm, Weston Turnville, in 1923. His companion, Thomas Fleet Edwards, died in January 1896 after falling in a ditch.

Mr. Partington, who never went back to his wife, returned to Manchester, the city of his birth, where he died in 1897. In his will he left £500 in trust to buy an annuity for Myfanwy, but he specified that this was to be forfeited if the terms of his will were disputed.

The Mensor Affair – the living resequestrated

The Rev. Dr. Meyer Mensor, a learned Jewish Rabbi, who was converted to Christianity in 1861, served Stoke Mandeville as vicar for 27 years. During that time he was involved in numerous disputes with both parishioners and the education authorities.

The period of his incumbency was one of great change in the country as a whole, with parishes losing a great deal of their traditional influence in such areas as health, roads, education and general administration. He probably felt he was fighting a justified battle against the forces of secular change.

But in his earlier days he and his wife, Annie Rose, were a generous couple and Mrs. Mensor's annual treats for the children and 'wives of the labourers' were always substantial. At Christmas time gifts of 'prime beef, tea and sugar were dispensed to all the impoverished widows, and the sick and needy, in the parish'. As time went by, however, Dr. Mensor became more and more eccentric. He took to wearing his university cap and gown on all occasions and in all weathers, and was never without his mortarboard, which became a symbol of his authority in his decreasing sphere of influence. To be fair, towards the end, Dr. and Mrs. Mensor had become a friendless and vulnerable old couple in an age when close association with others could not transcend the class barrier.

Very little is known of Mrs. Mensor, apart from the fact that she was born in Lincolnshire, and details of her marriage cannot be found in this country. The final blow for her husband came when she died in May 1906 aged 89, and was buried under the chancel of the church. The old man was left alone in a rapidly deteriorating vicarage.

Mrs. Mensor's niece, Elizabeth Hodson, aged 10 in 1881, had lived with them since childhood. Upon her marriage to a local labourer, John Rutland, the couple had taken up residence, rent free, in the unoccupied schoolmaster's house opposite the vicarage, on the understanding that John played the church organ every Sunday. As a temporary measure, after Mrs. Mensor's death, they took their uncle in while he advertised for a housekeeper. Although he was unsuccessful in this, he acquired a new wife from the advertisement and, just 10 weeks after the death of his first partner, married Mrs. Ellen Jeayes, a widowed lady, at Brighton parish church.

When the special licence was issued, Mensor gave some rather doubtful information to the authorities for the marriage certificate when he said that his deceased father's occupation was 'Major H. M. Army'. From what little is known of his past life in Prussia, the likelihood of his father being an officer in anybody's army is zero. Mrs Jeayes's attempt at gentility, in answer to the same question, was possibly more feasible – 'Barry O'Hara, gentleman'.

Meanwhile Stoke Mandeville church was closed, in the absence of a curate to take Sunday services, and soon tongues began to wag and quill pens to scratch. Francis, Lord Bishop of Oxford, who was on holiday at Clovelly in Devon, being advised of the position by Alfred Wheeler of Stoke House, wrote, 'Your letter made me very anxious', and he asked, 'How many Sundays within the past six months has there been no service?'. Schoolmaster Arnold answered this question: '... four whole Sundays this year as I remember: one in March or April on account of the illness of Mrs. Mensor, and two in July, the vicar being away in Brighton'.

It seems that, apart from the apparent neglect of duties, there had been an unpleasant scene at the *Bull's Head Hotel* in Aylesbury on the day of the newly-weds' return from Brighton. A shouting match, with much abuse and swearing, had resulted in the landlord ejecting them from the hotel. On another occasion in 1899, Mensor had behaved with 'unseemly violence' at a funeral. A more happy reception had been prepared in the village for the new Mrs. Mensor with flags hung across the Risborough Road from the elm trees which lined it.

Mensor was summoned to appear before the bishop to answer the charges, but failed to turn up on the appointed day. In a rather pathetic letter Mensor made his apologies:

> I am deeply sorrow [sorry] beyond measure that I did not keep the interview your Lordship so kindly granted me. My troubles are so great and deep that I forgot the reckoning of the days of the week. I thought today as Wednesday and was prepared to come to Oxford tomorrow, thinking tomorrow is Thursday. I call God to witness. I beg your Lordship will mercifully forgive me.

Archdeacon Kay at Lincoln became involved. He reported in October the contents of a letter from Mensor in which he had poured out his troubles:

> He ... says his wife made it her dying request that he should marry again at once owing to his need of care. It appears he advertised for a suitable housekeeper and, failing to obtain one, answered the advertisement of some unprincipled woman, married her and then was obliged to get rid of her.

A Commission of Enquiry was set up and evidence taken from 17 parties concerning the charges against the vicar, which included neglect of Sunday services and lack of visitation of the sick, as well as the ugly scene in Aylesbury. The new Mrs. Mensor had by this time gone off to London.

The report, whilst finding that the closure of the church was in some measure explained by the sudden illness of his wife, also noted that Mensor's behaviour had caused many of his parishioners to stay away from church so that, on one occasion the congregation consisted of three adults, and on another, service was not held in consequence of the absence of a congregation'. Many also felt strong objection to his second marriage so soon after the death of his first wife.

The enquiry's finding were '... that Dr. Mensor has inadequately performed ... but we think it right to add that he is now aged and generally feeble and his speech is hard to understand and may be liable to misconstruction'.

A further complication arose when Mrs. Rutland's parents, who had been invited down from Lincoln by Mensor to keep house for him, were evicted from the vicarage on his orders after he had thrown himself on the mercy of his wife and gone off to London to be looked after. Mrs. Rutland wrote that '...before they could get their things out [of the vicarage], he sent two men from London to put them out on the road without money or friends. They came to me and are dependent on me; still my husband earning only 13s. a week'.

The other side of the story was given to the bishop by Mrs. Ellen Mensor:

> ... his late wife's relatives had quite taken possession of the place and my husband's feeble mind had been quite powerless to prevent them. He came to me broken in mind and body followed by his late wife's niece who staggered into the place intoxicated ... they are very low people and used the most terrible language. I need not tell you as you are already aware what I suffered at the vicarage among this degraded class.

The Aylesbury solicitor advising the diocese was not far off the mark when he commented: 'I fear both parties are more anxious to acquire Dr Mensor's effects than to care for him'.

At the end of January, Mensor was hinting his willingness to resign the living but was anxious, before committing himself in writing, to safeguard any pension which might be coming his way from the Church Commissioners.

Then the news broke that the parish registers were missing. This was a serious civil matter and Somerset House, in particular 'is ablaze with excitement about the Stoke Mandeville registers'. This information was given to the diocesan office by the bishop's chaplain, the Rev. John M. C. Crum who, when the Act of Sequestration was published in January 1907, was appointed stipendiary curate at £2 2s. per week. The Act took the parish, including any income accruing, out of the incumbent's hands back into that of the diocese.

But the matter of the registers was still outstanding and as the *Victoria County History*, which was being compiled about this time, states, 'The registers are missing'. In fact they had been swept up with the rest of Dr. Mensor's library, and were residing in a pawnbroker's shop in London.

A further Commission of Enquiry had been set up and it found that Mensor was '... incapacitated ... bodily infirm from due performance of duties ... resignation under provisions of Incumbents' Resignation Acts of 1871 and 1877 expedient ... recommends a pension of £40 per annum out of the revenue of the benefice'.

Now that his pension had been safeguarded, although not actually paid, Dr. Mensor was willing to resign. But as far as the diocese was concerned the registers were still missing. When finally in December 1908 an advance of £5 was made, Mrs. Mensor could no longer prevaricate and dispatched the precious registers. As she delicately put it: 'Dr. Mensor was under the impression that he had already sent them. I should have seen it before but unfortunately the sack of books where they had been put had been stored away with other things. I had to get money before I could release them'.

Young Mr. Crum had the last word in the matter. Writing to the diocesan office he said, in a somewhat snide manner:

> I congratulate you on running to earth the registers. The old gentleman has cost a good deal of money one way and another. I wonder what the market value or pawn shop value of the books was. I am now settled here [Windsor] as curate. I suppose I ought to send my licence to be altered. I have it, unpawned, in my writing desk.

Mr. Crum sounds a supercilious young man although he went on to considerable Church preferment in later years.

And what of the Rev. Dr. Meyor Mensor? He lived for another five years in poverty and senility, and died in 1913 at the Hostel of God, Clapham Common. So ended a rather sad episode in the history of Stoke Mandeville.

Bibliography

The Aylesbury News and Bucks Advertiser

Borthwick Institute of Historical Research, York University, Ordination papers (1861)

Bucks County Record Office, D/BML; D/WIG; IR/9; IR/M/11; IR/C/196/1-11; DVD/1/79/; PU/A27-9; T/J/2, NM.110/3/1; D/Pc/309, S.M. Overseers of the Poor and S.M. Surveyors of the Highway

The Bucks Herald

Bucks Record Society, vol. 13, *Ship Money Papers* (1965)

Bucks Record Society, vol. 16, *Letter Books of Samuel Wilberforce* (1970)

Cocks, A. H., *The Church Bells of Buckinghamshire* (1897)

Crockfords Clerical Directories (1880-1918)

Dictionary of National Biography, vol. 11 (1892-3)

Eland, G., *In Bucks* (1923)

Keir, Sir D. L., *The Constitutional History of Modern Britain since 1485* (1969)

Kelly's Directory of Bucks

Lipscombe, G., *The History and Antiquities of the County of Buckinghamshire* vols. 2 & 3 (1847)

Matthaei, E. R., *History of Stoke Mandeville* (1955)

Mingay, Prof. G. E., *Rural life in Victorian England* (1976)

Morris, J., *Domesday Book: Buckinghamshire* (1978)

Oxford County Record Office, Diocesan Files

Pearce, R., *Stoke Mandeville – Past and Present.* Articles in the newsletters of the Stoke Mandeville Branch of the A.D.C. & U.A. (1971-7)

Priest, Rev. St John, *General View of the Agriculture of Buckinghamshire* (1810)

Principal Probate Registry Family Division, wills

Public Record Office ED.2; M.H.12; ED.10; ED.49; ED.6; HO.107; RG.9, 10, 11; IR.5B; H.O.129

'Records of Bucks', *Journal of the Bucks Archaeological Society* vol. 8 (1903) & vol. 18 (1916)

Registrar General, certificates of marriages and baptisms

Richardson, J., *Local Historian's Encyclopedia* (1987)

The Royal Commission on Historical Monuments – *Bucks (South)* vol. 2 (1912)

St Mary's, Stoke Mandeville, parish registers

Sheenan, J. J., *The History and Topography of Buckinghamshire* (1862)
Stoke Mandeville County Combined School, *School Logs*
Stoke Mandeville Parish Council, *Minute Books*
Stoke Mandeville Parish Meetings, *Minute Books*
Stoke Mandeville Women's Institute, *Minute Books*
The Times (1830)
Victoria County History – Buckinghamshire, vol. 2 (1908)

Index

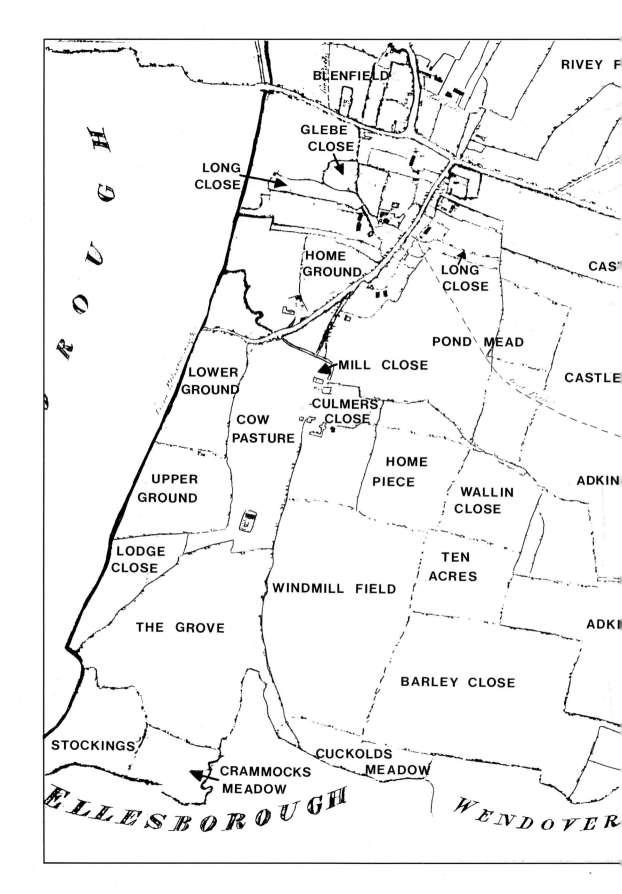